Titans of the Gilded Age: Power, Wealth, and the Making of Modern New York

Vanderbilt, Carnegie, Rockefeller & JP Morgan—the Tycoons Who Built Monopolies, Forged America's Economy, and Shaped a Nation's Future.

About the Author

Margaret Ellis

Margaret Ellis is a historian and writer with a passion for uncovering the stories of America's most transformative eras. With a background in American history and a particular interest in the societal and cultural shifts of the Gilded Age, Ellis brings the world of New York's elite to life, illuminating the figures and families whose wealth and influence helped shape modern America. Her extensive research and storytelling prowess offer readers a captivating journey into the heart of one of the most fascinating periods in American history.

Table of Contents

Introduction

In the grand marble halls of Caroline Astor's Fifth Avenue mansion on a January evening in 1883, New York's elite gathered for what would become one of the most defining moments of the Gilded Age. As the city's wealthiest and most powerful families arrived in their carriages, they were about to witness the culmination of an unprecedented transformation in American society – one that had turned a young republic into the world's leading industrial power, created fortunes of unimaginable magnitude, and forever changed the face of New York City.

The story of America's Gilded Age is more than a tale of extraordinary wealth and extravagant displays of prosperity. It is the story of how a handful of remarkable individuals – some born into privilege, others rising from humble beginnings – shaped the very foundation of modern America. Through their ambitions, innovations, and often controversial methods, figures like Cornelius Vanderbilt, John D. Rockefeller, Andrew Carnegie, J.P. Morgan, and the Astor family not only amassed unprecedented fortunes but also revolutionized industry, finance, and philanthropy in ways that continue to influence our world today.

In the span of a single generation, these titans transformed New York from a growing commercial center into the world's financial capital. They built railways that connected the continent, forged steel empires that industrialized the nation, created banking systems that would define modern finance, and established philanthropic institutions that continue to shape American society. Their legacies stand today in the towering skyscrapers of Manhattan, the great cultural institutions that line Fifth Avenue, and the universities and libraries that bear their names.

Yet their story is also one of stark contrasts. While the elite dined from golden plates in their Newport "cottages," immigrants crowded into tenements just blocks from Fifth Avenue's mansions. As industrial fortunes grew to unprecedented sizes, workers faced dangerous conditions and grueling hours in factories and mines. This tension between progress and inequality, between innovation and exploitation, defined the era and continues to resonate with our own time.

Through personal letters, contemporary accounts, and detailed records, we'll explore how these remarkable individuals built their empires, wielded their influence, and ultimately shaped the American Dream. We'll witness their triumphs and failures, their feuds and alliances, and how their actions continue to influence our understanding of wealth, power, and social responsibility.

As we examine their lives and legacies, we'll discover that the questions raised during the Gilded Age – about the concentration of wealth, the relationship between private power and public good, and the responsibilities of the extremely wealthy to society – remain strikingly relevant today. In many ways, understanding the titans of the Gilded Age is key to understanding our own era of technological revolution, economic transformation, and growing inequality.

The story begins in the aftermath of the Civil War, as America stood on the brink of its greatest period of industrial expansion. New technologies, vast natural resources, and an influx of ambitious immigrants would provide the raw materials for unprecedented growth. But it would take the vision, ambition, and often ruthless determination of a remarkable group of individuals to forge these elements into the modern American economy. This is their story – a tale of ambition and innovation, of rivalry and reform, that shaped not just New York City but the very nature of American capitalism itself.

Chapter One

Vanderbilt Unleashed — The Ruthless Rise of America's First Corporate King

"Power is the great aphrodisiac." – Cornelius Vanderbilt. On a bitter January morning in 1870, Cornelius Vanderbilt stood at the window of his Manhattan office, watching as smoke billowed from the locomotives at his newly consolidated New York Central Railroad. The seventy-five-year-old 'Commodore,' as he was known throughout Wall Street, had just completed the largest corporate merger in American history to that point, creating a transportation empire that would revolutionize American business forever.

The empire Vanderbilt was building would fundamentally reshape American business and society, creating a template for corporate consolidation that would define the Gilded Age. His story embodied the raw ambition and ruthless determination that characterized America's first generation of industrial titans. From humble beginnings as a ferry operator on Staten Island, Vanderbilt had clawed his way to the pinnacle of American business through a combination of shrewd innovation and bare-knuckled competition.

The transformation of his New York Central Railroad into America's first great corporate giant marked a pivotal moment in business history. Through masterful consolidation of competing lines and aggressive expansion, Vanderbilt created an integrated transportation network that helped knit together a rapidly industrializing nation. His methods – both admired and feared – would become a blueprint for the robber barons who followed.

Nowhere was Vanderbilt's mastery of power more evident than in the legendary "Harlem Corner" of 1863. When corrupt New York City Council members attempted to profit by short-selling Harlem Railroad stock after secretly planning to revoke the company's street railway franchise, Vanderbilt orchestrated a brilliant counter-strike. Quietly accumulating every available share, he waited as the Council's decision became public. When the short-sellers desperately rushed to cover their positions, they found Vanderbilt controlling the entire market. The stock price exploded from $3 to $285 per share, bankrupting the conspirators and cementing Vanderbilt's reputation as a financial genius not to be trifled with.

This episode revealed not just Vanderbilt's tactical brilliance but also the deep corruption that pervaded New York's political and financial systems during the era. The incident led to significant reforms in stock market regulations and established new precedents for corporate governance. More importantly, it demonstrated how the emerging class of industrial titans could outmaneuver even the political establishment, shifting the balance of power in American society.

As Vanderbilt gazed out at his railroad empire that January morning, he represented a new kind of American power – one based not on land or political office, but on control of the vital arteries of commerce and industry. His consolidation of the New York Central would serve as a model for future industrial organization, while his methods of vertical integration and strategic monopoly would become standard business practices. The massive wealth he accumulated – over $100 million by the time of his death – would establish his family among New York's elite for generations to come.

The 'Commodore,' as he was known on Wall Street, was more than just a successful businessman; he was a harbinger of a new economic order. His rise signaled the dawn of the modern corporation and the emergence of a new American aristocracy built on industrial wealth rather than inherited privilege. The massive fortune he accumulated would help transform New York City itself, funding landmarks like Grand Central Depot that reshaped Manhattan's landscape and established patterns of urban development that persist to this day.

As the smoke from his locomotives drifted over the Manhattan skyline, it carried with it the promise and peril of this new industrial age – an era of unprecedented growth and opportunity, but also one of increasing consolidation of wealth and power in the hands of a few. Vanderbilt's story was just beginning, but it would set the stage for decades of dramatic change in American business, society, and culture.

From Staten Island Ferry to Railroad King: Vanderbilt's Early Business Evolution

"I have been insane on the subject of moneymaking all my life." - Cornelius Vanderbilt, 1850

On a brisk autumn morning in 1810, sixteen-year-old Cornelius Vanderbilt stood at the helm of his newly acquired periauger, a small sailing vessel purchased with $100 borrowed from his mother. [1,2,4] The Staten Island shoreline stretched before him as he prepared for his first independent ferry crossing to Manhattan, a journey that would mark the beginning of one of the most remarkable business transformations in American history.

The young Vanderbilt's early ferry service was a study in calculated efficiency. He charged lower fares than his competitors while maintaining strict punctuality, earning the loyalty of working-class passengers who relied on his service for their daily commute. [1,2] His periauger, though humble, became known for its reliability, even in treacherous weather when other operators remained docked. This dedication to service would become a hallmark of his business philosophy, even as his enterprises grew to unprecedented scale.

In 1817, a pivotal opportunity arose when Thomas Gibbons, a wealthy steamboat operator, noticed the young entrepreneur's success. Gibbons offered Vanderbilt a position as captain of his steamboat service, which was then challenging the powerful monopoly held by Robert Fulton and Robert Livingston. [1,3] The partnership thrust

Vanderbilt into one of the most significant legal battles in American business history – Gibbons v. Ogden. The Supreme Court's 1824 decision striking down state-sanctioned monopolies would later provide the legal foundation for Vanderbilt's own expansion strategies. [3,4]

Working under Gibbons, Vanderbilt mastered the intricacies of steamboat operations while developing his understanding of corporate strategy. [1,3] He learned the art of legal maneuvering, the importance of political connections, and the power of controlling vital transportation routes. When Gibbons died in 1826, Vanderbilt was prepared to launch his own steamboat empire. [1,2,3]

The creation of his Dispatch Line between New York and Philadelphia demonstrated Vanderbilt's ruthless business acumen. He slashed fares to levels that seemed impossible to match, forcing competitors into ruinous price wars. [1,2] When they could no longer sustain losses, they would inevitably approach Vanderbilt with buyout offers. This pattern of aggressive competition followed by profitable consolidation would become his signature strategy, earning him both admiration and resentment throughout the business world.

The California Gold Rush of 1849 presented Vanderbilt with his next great opportunity. While others focused on mining, he recognized the real fortune lay in transportation. His Accessory Transit Company, offering passage to California via Nicaragua, cut weeks off the traditional Panama route. [1,3,4] The venture proved so profitable that competitors paid him $40,000 monthly to cease operations in certain regions, demonstrating the extraordinary power he had accumulated. [3,4]

By the late 1850s, Vanderbilt began noticing a shift in transportation technology. The expanding railroad network threatened to revolutionize American commerce. Rather than resist this change, he embraced it, gradually selling his steamboat interests and investing heavily in railroads. This strategic pivot would ultimately lead to the creation of the New York Central Railroad system, transforming him from 'Commodore' to 'Railroad King'. [1,4,5]

Vanderbilt's evolution from Staten Island ferry operator to railroad tycoon fundamentally shaped modern American business practices. His methods of vertical integration, strategic consolidation, and competitive pricing became standard tactics in corporate America. [1,4] The legal precedents established during his battles against monopolies continue to influence antitrust law today. Perhaps most significantly, his career demonstrated how technological innovation and adaptive business strategies could create unprecedented wealth and power in America's free market system.

As I stand at the modern Staten Island Ferry terminal, watching the massive orange vessels cross New York Harbor, I'm struck by how Vanderbilt's legacy endures. The free ferry service now operating on his old route serves as a reminder of how far American transportation has come, while the towering skyscrapers of Manhattan's financial district stand as monuments to the corporate empire he helped pioneer. His journey from humble ferryman to railroad king remains one of the most compelling stories of American business transformation, illustrating both the opportunities and ethical challenges of unfettered capitalism.

The Great Railroad Wars: Consolidation and Competition

"Competition brings out the best in products and the worst in people." - John D. Rockefeller, 1902

On a frigid morning in January 1877, a solitary locomotive's whistle pierced the winter air as it pulled into the Baltimore & Ohio Railroad yard in Martinsburg, West Virginia. The engineer, his face gaunt from months of reduced wages, knew that this day would mark a turning point in American labor history. The railroad company had just announced its third wage cut in a year – a 10% reduction that would push many workers' families to the brink of starvation. [6,12,15]

The Great Railroad Strike of 1877 erupted like a powder keg, spreading rapidly across the nation's rail networks. In Pittsburgh, workers and citizens united in their fury against the Pennsylvania Railroad, setting fire to railcars and depots, leaving parts of the city in ruins. [6,15] The violence reflected the deep-seated tensions between railroad barons, who had amassed unprecedented wealth, and their workers, who struggled to feed their families on meager wages. [6,12]

Meanwhile, in the opulent offices of New York's financial district, railroad titans like Cornelius Vanderbilt orchestrated massive consolidations that would reshape American business forever. [8,11] The New York Central Railroad, formed through the merger of ten smaller companies, demonstrated how strategic consolidation could create efficiency and profit – though often at the cost of local autonomy and worker welfare. [7,9]

The Pennsylvania Railroad, under the shrewd leadership of its executives, embarked on an ambitious campaign of absorption, eventually controlling over 600 smaller lines by 1900. [7,9,13] This consolidation brought standardization to the industry – unified gauge tracks, coordinated schedules, and improved safety measures. [9 13] Yet it also concentrated immense power in the hands of a few corporate leaders.

Rate wars between competing railroads turned the industry into a battlefield of economic warfare. Companies slashed prices to unsustainable levels, driving smaller competitors into bankruptcy before raising rates again once competition had been eliminated. [13] These practices led to public outcry and eventually sparked the creation of the Interstate Commerce Act of 1887 – America's first significant federal regulatory legislation. [13]

The human cost of this corporate warfare was staggering. In one particularly poignant incident during the 1877 strike, federal troops opened fire on protesters in Pittsburgh, killing 20 civilians. [6,15] The scene of soldiers firing on American workers shocked the nation and crystallized growing concerns about the concentration of corporate power.

Yet amid this turmoil, the railroads were transforming America in unprecedented ways. The expansion of rail networks knit the nation together, enabling the rise of national markets and standardized time zones. [14] Cities along major rail routes flourished, while those bypassed often withered. The power to determine a community's economic fate often rested in the boardrooms of New York's railroad barons.

As I walk through Grand Central Terminal today, I'm struck by how the echoes of these railroad wars still reverberate through American society. The building itself, a testament to the wealth and vision of the Vanderbilt empire, stands as a monument to both the grandeur and the contradictions of the Gilded Age. The consolidation strategies pioneered by railroad magnates became the template for modern corporate mergers. [7,10] Their battles with labor helped shape American worker protection laws, while their monopolistic practices led to antitrust legislation that still governs business competition. [7,10,13]

Perhaps most significantly, the railroad wars marked America's transformation from a collection of local economies into an integrated national market – a change that fundamentally altered not just commerce, but the very fabric of American society. [14] The tension between corporate power and public interest, so dramatically displayed during the railroad wars, continues to define American economic debates today. As modern corporations grow to sizes that would astound even the railroad barons, we still grapple with many of the same questions about competition, regulation, and the balance between private profit and public good that emerged during those turbulent years of railroad consolidation.

Innovation in Corporate Structure: The Birth of the Modern Corporation

"The growth of corporate power has far outstripped our conception of its scope." - William Vanderbilt, 1879

On one particular autumn morning in 1869, the directors of the newly consolidated New York Central and Hudson River Railroad gathered in Cornelius Vanderbilt's opulent Madison Avenue mansion. The meeting would mark a pivotal moment in American business history – the birth of the modern corporation. As they sat around the mahogany table in Vanderbilt's study, these men were about to create something unprecedented: A business entity larger and more complex than anything that had come before. [16,17,4]

The New York Central's consolidation represented a watershed moment in corporate evolution. Through careful legal maneuvering and strategic acquisitions, Vanderbilt had united ten previously independent railroads into a single, integrated system. This new enterprise required novel approaches to management, financing, and operations that would reshape American business forever. [16,17,4]

In the basement offices of the railroad's headquarters, an army of clerks and accountants developed revolutionary systems to track the movement of hundreds of trains, thousands of employees, and millions of dollars. The sheer scale of operations demanded new forms of organizational structure. Department heads emerged to manage specific functions – maintenance, scheduling, accounting – creating the first modern corporate bureaucracy. These innovations in management would soon be adopted by other industries, from steel to oil. [19]

Meanwhile, in the marble-clad corridors of Wall Street, another revolution was unfolding. The unprecedented capital requirements of railroad corporations spurred innovations in finance. Investment banks like J.P. Morgan & Co. pioneered new methods of raising money through stock and bond issues. The New York Stock Exchange saw its daily trading volume explode as railroad securities became the first widely traded corporate stocks. [19]

Yet this transformation came at a human cost. In the railyards of Albany and Buffalo, workers struggled with 12-hour days and dangerous conditions while corporate profits soared. The contrast was stark: as Vanderbilt's personal fortune approached $100 million, his brakemen earned barely a dollar a day. This disparity would eventually spark some of the era's most violent labor conflicts. [18,19]

The legal framework for this new corporate order was established in landmark cases like Dartmouth College v. Woodward and Santa Clara County v. Southern Pacific Railroad, which granted corporations many of the rights of individual citizens while protecting shareholders through limited liability. These decisions created the legal foundation for the modern corporation's tremendous accumulation of wealth and power. [14,19]

Perhaps most significantly, the rise of the corporation fundamentally altered the relationship between business and government. As railroad corporations grew to rival states in size and influence, they began wielding unprecedented political power. The famous "Erie War" of 1868 demonstrated how corporate interests could manipulate both markets and legislatures, leading to calls for greater regulation. [19]

Walking through the restored grandeur of Grand Central Terminal today, I'm struck by how thoroughly the innovations of this era still shape our world. The organizational structures pioneered by the railroads remain the template for modern multinational corporations. The relationship between Wall Street and corporate America, first forged in railroad financing, continues to drive our economy. Even our modern debates about corporate power and responsibility echo the concerns first raised during this transformative period. [17,4]

The birth of the modern corporation during the Gilded Age fundamentally reshaped American society, creating new forms of wealth and power while establishing institutional structures that persist to this day. As we grapple with questions about corporate influence, worker rights, and economic inequality in our own time, we would do well to remember the lessons of this pivotal era when the framework of modern American capitalism first emerged. [19]

The legacy of this corporate revolution extends far beyond business practices. It transformed American society itself, creating new social classes, reshaping cities, and establishing patterns of wealth concentration that continue to influence economic inequality today. The modern corporation, born in the boardrooms and rail yards of the Gilded Age, remains one of the most powerful and enduring innovations of American capitalism. [18,19]

The Harlem Corner: Stock Market Manipulation and Wall Street Tactics

"The stock market is a device for transferring money from the impatient to the patient." - Cornelius Vanderbilt, 1863

It was on a crisp spring morning in 1863, when the marble halls of the New York Stock Exchange echoed with frantic shouts as traders scrambled to respond to an unprecedented financial crisis. The Harlem Railroad stock, which had been trading at a modest $3 per share just months earlier, was now soaring past $100 and climbing higher by the hour. [17,8] At the center of this financial maelstrom stood Cornelius Vanderbilt, orchestrating what would become known as one of the most audacious market manipulations in Wall Street history.

The drama had begun when Vanderbilt learned of a secret plot by members of the New York City Council. These corrupt officials had conspired to revoke the Harlem Railroad's franchise to operate horse-drawn streetcars on Manhattan's streets. [19] Their plan was simple but devious: Short-sell Harlem stock before announcing their decision, then profit from the inevitable price collapse when the news became public.

But Vanderbilt, already a seasoned master of market manipulation, recognized an opportunity for what he called a 'corner' – buying up virtually every available share of stock while simultaneously encouraging short-sellers to bet against it. [17,21] As the Council members and their Wall Street allies borrowed and sold more shares than actually existed, Vanderbilt quietly accumulated an iron grip on the market.

When the Council finally announced their decision to revoke the franchise, expecting to profit from a market crash, they instead found themselves trapped in Vanderbilt's carefully laid snare. [19,21] The stock price, rather than plummeting, began to rise astronomically as short-sellers desperately tried to buy shares to cover their positions. With Vanderbilt controlling nearly all available stock, they had no choice but to pay whatever price he demanded.

The scene at the Exchange that morning captured the raw essence of Gilded Age capitalism. [20,19] As the stock price rocketed past $285 per share, ruined speculators slumped against the building's classical columns while others frantically waved trading slips in the air, their faces contorted with desperation. One prominent trader, upon realizing the extent of his losses, reportedly collapsed on the trading floor, his fortune evaporated in a matter of hours.

Vanderbilt's triumph in the Harlem Corner demonstrated not just his tactical brilliance but also the dangerous concentration of power in the hands of the era's financial titans. [21] The episode exposed the deep corruption within New York's political system and the vulnerability of markets to manipulation by wealthy operators. [19] It marked a crucial turning point in American financial history, leading to calls for greater regulation and oversight of stock market practices.

The aftermath of the Harlem Corner reverberated through Wall Street for decades. The incident established new precedents for corporate governance and market manipulation, while also highlighting the need for more robust financial regulations. [20,19] Vanderbilt's tactics, though legal at the time, would later be outlawed through securities regulations designed to prevent such extreme market manipulation.

As I stand on Wall Street today, watching traders hurry past the same Greek Revival facade of the New York Stock Exchange, I'm struck by how the echoes of the Harlem Corner still resonate in modern finance. While regulations now prohibit the most blatant forms of market manipulation, the fundamental tensions between private profit and public interest that Vanderbilt's scheme exposed continue to shape our financial markets. [20]

The legacy of the Harlem Corner extends far beyond its immediate impact on Wall Street. It marked a crucial step in the evolution of American capitalism, demonstrating both the innovative potential and destructive power of unregulated financial markets. [17,21] The episode helped establish New York as the nation's financial capital while also planting the seeds for the regulatory frameworks that would eventually emerge to govern modern markets.

Perhaps most importantly, the Harlem Corner illustrated how the concentration of wealth and power in the hands of industrial titans could fundamentally reshape not just markets but the very fabric of American society. [20,19] As we continue to grapple with questions of financial regulation, market manipulation, and the proper balance between private enterprise and public good, the lessons of Vanderbilt's audacious gambit remain remarkably relevant to our contemporary debates about the role of finance in American life.

Building Grand Central Depot: Reshaping Manhattan's Landscape

"The public be damned! I'm working for my stockholders." - William Henry Vanderbilt, 1882

As the first rays of sunlight pierced through the smoky Manhattan air one October morning in 1869, Cornelius Vanderbilt stood at the corner of 42nd Street and Fourth Avenue, surveying the vast expanse of land before him. The Commodore's weathered face betrayed no emotion as he contemplated the ambitious vision taking shape in his mind – a magnificent railway terminal that would reshape Manhattan's landscape forever.

The site was a chaos of activity. Hundreds of laborers toiled in the early morning chill, their picks and shovels biting into Manhattan's bedrock. The construction of Grand Central Depot had begun, marking the most ambitious architectural undertaking of its era. The project would cost $6.4 million – an astronomical sum that only Vanderbilt's immense fortune could support. [22,28]

The transformation of this once-peripheral area was met with fierce resistance from the wealthy residents of nearby Fifth Avenue. They viewed the incursion of industrial infrastructure into their exclusive neighborhood with horror. One prominent society matron was reported to have declared at a dinner party, 'Mr. Vanderbilt may have his millions, but he cannot buy our silence!' Yet Vanderbilt pressed forward, wielding legal 'seizure rights' with characteristic ruthlessness to secure the necessary properties. [23,28]

Architect John B. Snook's design for the depot embodied the grandeur of the Second Empire style, rivaling the great European terminals of London and Paris. [22,23,28] The three-story L-shaped headhouse, faced in gleaming brick and crowned with a mansard roof, would stand as a monument to American progress. The vast train shed, with its revolutionary glass-and-iron balloon roof spanning 530 feet, would shelter passengers from the elements while allowing smoke from the steam locomotives to escape. [22,28]

Yet beneath the architectural splendor lay a stark reality. The same laborers who built this temple of transportation struggled to survive on meager wages. They worked dangerous twelve-hour shifts, scaling precarious heights to install the massive glass panels of the train shed roof. Many lived in nearby tenements, their families crowded into dark, airless rooms while the depot rose as a symbol of Gilded Age excess.

The depot's opening in October 1871 marked a turning point in New York's history. For the first time, passengers could access three major railroads – the New York Central, the Harlem, and the New Haven – from a single terminal. The amenities were unprecedented: four restaurants, a billiards room, elegant shops, and even a dedicated police station. [22] It was a microcosm of Gilded Age society, where first-class passengers lounged in luxurious waiting rooms while immigrants and working-class travelers crowded onto wooden benches in separate areas.

However, the triumph of Grand Central Depot was not without its dark side. The smoke-filled Park Avenue tunnel became notorious for accidents, culminating in a tragic collision in 1902 that claimed fifteen lives. [27,28] The disaster forced a reckoning with the limitations of steam power in an urban environment, eventually leading to the electrification of the railways and the construction of the even grander Grand Central Terminal.

As I walk through today's Grand Central Terminal, I'm amazed by how Vanderbilt's vision continues to shape Manhattan. The depot's construction sparked the development of Park Avenue and the surrounding neighborhoods, transforming what was once the city's periphery into its beating heart. [22,23] The architectural ambition of Grand Central Depot set a precedent for the marriage of commerce and culture that defines New York to this day.

The legacy of Grand Central Depot extends far beyond its physical footprint. It demonstrated how private wealth could reshape public spaces, establishing a pattern that would be repeated throughout American cities. The tension between progress and preservation, between corporate power and community interests, that marked its construction continues to influence urban development debates today. [25,26] In many ways, the story of Grand Central Depot encapsulates the essence of the Gilded Age itself – a period when ambitious visions and ruthless determination transformed America's urban landscape, leaving an indelible mark on our cities and society that persists into the twenty-first century. [22,24,25]

Legacy of the Commodore: Impact on Modern Business Practices

"The public be damned! I'm working for my stockholders." - William Henry Vanderbilt, 1882

As I stand in the marble-clad boardroom of the New York Central Railroad's headquarters, the legacy of Cornelius Vanderbilt's business empire stretches before me like the steel rails of his vast network. The Commodore's death the previous year (January 4th, 1877) marked not just the passing of America's richest man, but the end of an era in American business. His $100 million fortune – equivalent to billions in today's dollars – represented more than mere wealth; it embodied a revolution in how business would be conducted for generations to come.

Vanderbilt's most enduring impact lay in his pioneering approach to corporate consolidation. Through the merger of the New York Central and Hudson River railroads, he demonstrated how combining competing enterprises could create unprecedented efficiency and scale. [3,30,33] This strategy of consolidation would become the template for industrial giants like Standard Oil and U.S. Steel, fundamentally reshaping American capitalism. His methods of vertical integration – controlling every aspect of his business from track to terminal – established patterns still evident in modern corporate structures.

In the bustling freight yards of Albany, I witness the practical application of another Vanderbilt innovation – systematic cost-cutting and competitive pricing. The Commodore's ruthless efficiency in reducing operational expenses while undercutting competitors' rates transformed transportation economics. [29,32] These tactics, though brutal in their impact on smaller operators, established principles of market competition that continue to influence modern business strategy. Companies like Walmart and Amazon would later employ similar approaches to dominate their respective markets.

The magnificence of Grand Central Depot stands as perhaps the most visible testament to Vanderbilt's impact on urban development. His vision of integrating transportation infrastructure with commercial and residential growth helped create the modern American city. [32] The development of Manhattan's Park Avenue corridor, sparked by the terminal's construction, demonstrated how private enterprise could reshape urban landscapes – a pattern repeated countless times in cities across America.

Yet beneath the gleaming surface of Vanderbilt's success lay darker implications. His monopolistic practices and brutal treatment of labor would eventually spark public outrage and government intervention. The Sherman Antitrust Act of 1890, though enacted after his death, was a direct response to the type of corporate consolidation he pioneered. [31,33] His famous declaration 'The public be damned!' – actually uttered by his son William – encapsulated an attitude toward corporate responsibility that would haunt American business for generations.

Vanderbilt's influence extended beyond mere business practices. His emphasis on operational efficiency and disciplined corporate culture established standards that would define American management for decades. The centralized decision-making structure he implemented at the New York Central became a model for corporate organization, while his focus on shareholder value over personal enrichment – unusual for his era – helped establish modern principles of corporate governance. [30]

Perhaps most significantly, Vanderbilt's career embodied the transformation of American capitalism from an entrepreneurial to a corporate model. His evolution from independent operator to corporate titan paralleled the nation's economic development. [3,8] The systems and structures he created – from corporate hierarchies to stock market practices – laid the groundwork for modern American business.

As I conclude my visit to the New York Central offices, I'm struck by how thoroughly Vanderbilt's legacy permeates contemporary business culture. His innovations in corporate structure, competitive strategy, and urban development continue to influence how American business operates. The tension between private profit and public good that characterized his career remains at the heart of ongoing debates about corporate power and responsibility.

The Commodore's lasting impact on American business practices extends far beyond the railroad empire he built. His methods of consolidation, competitive pricing, and corporate organization became the template for industrial capitalism. [30,32] While some of his more aggressive tactics have been tempered by regulation, the fundamental principles he established – efficiency, scale, and market dominance – continue to drive American business strategy. In many ways, modern corporate America remains the house that Vanderbilt built. The legacy of Cornelius Vanderbilt and the birth of modern corporate America marked a pivotal transformation in the nation's history. As the smoke cleared from the Harlem Corner and the magnificent Grand Central Depot rose above 42nd Street, a new era of American capitalism had dawned – one that would reshape not just New York, but the entire nation.

Vanderbilt's remarkable journey from Staten Island ferry operator to railroad titan embodied the raw ambition and ruthless determination that would come to define the Gilded Age. Through strategic consolidation, innovative corporate structures, and bare-knuckled competition, he created a template for industrial empire-building that subsequent generations would follow. The New York Central Railroad's emergence as America's first great corporate giant demonstrated how concentrated wealth and power could reshape both the physical and economic landscape of a rapidly industrializing nation.

Yet the Commodore's legacy was not without its dark side. The same business practices that built his fortune – monopolistic control, stock manipulation, and ruthless elimination of competition – sparked growing public concern about corporate power. The contrast between his immense wealth and the struggles of his workers highlighted the stark inequalities of the era. When his employees earned barely a dollar a day while he amassed $100 million, the seeds of future labor conflicts were sown.

The transformation of Manhattan's landscape through projects like Grand Central Depot illustrated how private wealth could reshape public spaces, establishing patterns of urban development that persist to this day. The elegant terminal, with its Second Empire grandeur, stood as a physical embodiment of the new corporate order – a place where first-class passengers lounged in luxury while immigrants and laborers crowded onto wooden benches in segregated waiting areas.

Perhaps most significantly, Vanderbilt's career marked America's transition from an entrepreneurial to a corporate economy. The organizational structures he pioneered – from hierarchical management to strategic consolidation – became the foundation of modern business practice. His emphasis on operational efficiency and shareholder value helped establish principles of corporate governance that continue to influence American capitalism.

As we examine today's debates about corporate power, income inequality, and the proper balance between private enterprise and public good, the echoes of Vanderbilt's era resonate clearly. The tension between innovation and monopoly, between progress and equity, that characterized his career remains at the heart of our economic discussions. Modern tech giants employing strategies of market dominance would be familiar to the Commodore, while contemporary concerns about corporate influence in politics mirror those raised during his lifetime.

In many ways, the story of Cornelius Vanderbilt is the story of modern American capitalism itself – a tale of unprecedented innovation and wealth creation, but also of social displacement and economic inequality. His legacy reminds us that the fundamental questions about power, progress, and prosperity that emerged during the Gilded Age continue to shape our society today. As new industrial titans rise in our own time, the lessons of Vanderbilt's era remain startlingly relevant to our ongoing dialogue about the future of American capitalism.

As the sun sets behind the gleaming spires of Manhattan, I'm fascinated by how thoroughly Vanderbilt's vision transformed this island. The corporate structures he created, the urban landscapes he shaped, and the economic principles he established continue to influence American life. In understanding his story – both its triumphs and its contradictions – we gain crucial insight into the forces that continue to shape our modern world.

Chapter Two

Black Gold Dynasty: John D. Rockefeller and the Standard Oil Monopoly

In 1870, as kerosene lamps illuminated America's homes, John D. Rockefeller surveyed the chaotic oil fields of Pennsylvania with calculating precision, envisioning an empire where others saw only disorder. Through his newly formed Standard Oil Company, the methodical thirty-one-year-old was about to embark on the most ambitious campaign of industrial consolidation the world had ever seen. "Competition is a sin," Rockefeller once declared, and his actions in the decades that followed would prove his unwavering commitment to this philosophy. As he methodically built Standard Oil into America's most formidable monopoly, his calculated strategies would forever transform American industry and set new precedents for corporate power.

From his earliest days in the oil business, Rockefeller displayed an almost religious dedication to organization and efficiency. His company's operations were a marvel of vertical integration, controlling everything from oil wells and refineries to barrel manufacturing and transportation. This obsession with control extended to his legendary bookkeeping practices, where every penny was accounted for with ruthless precision. Yet beneath this facade of methodical business practices lay a cutthroat determination to eliminate all competition.

The infamous Cleveland Massacre of 1872 demonstrated both Rockefeller's tactical brilliance and his merciless approach to competition. Through secret agreements with railroads, he secured preferential shipping rates that gave Standard Oil an insurmountable advantage over rivals. When he approached Cleveland's independent refiners with his ultimatum – sell out or face ruin – he orchestrated one of the most dramatic consolidations of industrial power in American history. Within just three months, twenty-two of Cleveland's twenty-six refineries had either sold to Standard Oil or shuttered their doors forever.

The case of Charles Watson became emblematic of Rockefeller's tactics. When Watson refused Standard Oil's initial buyout offer,

Rockefeller's agents informed him that they could ship oil at rates forty percent lower than what Watson paid. The message was clear: resist and face certain bankruptcy. Like many others, Watson ultimately capitulated, selling his life's work for a fraction of its value. This episode sent shockwaves through the industry and demonstrated how railroad rebates could be weaponized to build monopolistic power.

By 1880, Standard Oil controlled approximately 90 percent of America's oil refining capacity, an achievement that would make Rockefeller the world's first billionaire. Yet this unprecedented concentration of economic power sparked growing public outrage and eventually led to landmark antitrust legislation. The Sherman Antitrust Act of 1890 was largely written in response to Standard Oil's dominance, though it would take another two decades before the Supreme Court finally ordered the company's dissolution in 1911.

The legacy of Standard Oil and Rockefeller's ruthless business practices continues to shape American capitalism today. His innovative organizational methods, vertical integration strategies, and emphasis on efficiency became models for modern corporations. Yet his monopolistic practices also led to the development of antitrust laws that still govern business competition. The tension between corporate efficiency and market competition that Rockefeller embodied remains at the heart of ongoing debates about economic regulation and corporate power in America.

The Cleveland Beginning: Rockefeller's Early Business Ventures and Standard Oil's Formation

"I believe in the dignity of labor, whether with head or hand; that the world owes no man a living but that it owes every man an opportunity to make a living." - John D. Rockefeller

In 1855, sixteen-year-old John D. Rockefeller walked purposefully through Cleveland's bustling streets toward his first job interview. The young man had spent six weeks methodically visiting every bank, merchant, and commission house in the city, meticulously recording each interaction in a small leather notebook. This persistence would become his hallmark, transforming a bookkeeper's position at Hewitt & Tuttle into the foundation of an empire.

Rockefeller's early years in Cleveland revealed the methodical nature that would define his business career. Working as an assistant bookkeeper for 50 cents a day, [37] he approached his duties with religious devotion, treating each entry in the ledger as a sacred trust. "I had learned the underlying principles of business as a clerk," he later recalled, "and I believed I could handle them on a larger scale."

In 1859, the same year that Edwin Drake struck oil in Titusville, Pennsylvania, [34,36] Rockefeller took his first step toward independence. With $1,000 in savings and an equal loan from his father, he partnered with Maurice Clark to form a commission merchant business. [31,36] The timing proved fortuitous as Cleveland's strategic location between the oil fields of Pennsylvania and the markets of the West positioned it perfectly for the coming petroleum boom.

The Civil War years brought unprecedented opportunity. While others saw chaos in the rapidly expanding oil industry, Rockefeller recognized patterns and possibilities. In 1863, he and Clark invested in their first refinery with chemist Samuel Andrews, establishing Andrews, Clark & Company. [34,36] The venture proved immediately profitable, but Rockefeller's vision extended far beyond a single refinery.

A pivotal moment came in 1865 when tensions with the Clark brothers reached a breaking point. At a tense auction, Rockefeller bid $72,500 to buy out his partners' share in the refinery. It was a massive sum for the time, but Rockefeller never hesitated. "It was the day that determined my career," he later wrote. [31,34] The newly renamed Rockefeller & Andrews began a period of rapid expansion that would reshape American industry.

The formation of Standard Oil in 1870 marked the beginning of a new era in American business. With initial capital of $1 million, Rockefeller assembled a team of partners including his brother William, Samuel Andrews, Henry Flagler, and Stephen Harkness. [32,3] The company's name reflected Rockefeller's obsession with quality and standardization [32] – a revolutionary concept in an industry known for wildly varying product quality.

Rockefeller's approach to business was revolutionary. While competitors focused solely on refining, Standard Oil vertically integrated its operations, controlling everything from barrel manufacturing to transportation. [36] The company's laboratories developed uses for petroleum byproducts that others discarded as waste. Even the gasoline that refiners typically dumped into rivers was stored by Standard Oil, anticipating future uses. [36,37]

By 1872, Standard Oil controlled nearly all of Cleveland's refining capacity through a combination of buyouts and strategic partnerships. The infamous "Cleveland Massacre" saw twenty-two of the city's twenty-six refineries absorbed into Standard Oil's growing empire. [31,34] While critics decried these tactics as ruthless, Rockefeller saw them as necessary to bring order to a chaotic industry.

The legacy of Rockefeller's Cleveland beginnings continues to shape American business today. His innovations in corporate organization, vertical integration, and efficiency standards became templates for modern corporations. [32,35] The antitrust legislation created to check Standard Oil's power still governs business competition. Perhaps most significantly, Rockefeller's example of systematic organization and professional management transformed American capitalism from a haphazard pursuit into a scientific enterprise.

In many ways, modern corporate America was born in those early Cleveland years. The tension between efficiency and competition, monopoly and free markets, and private power and public good that Rockefeller's rise embodied continues to define our economic debates. [33,36] As we grapple with questions of corporate consolidation and market power in our own time, the lessons of Rockefeller's Cleveland beginnings remain startlingly relevant.

The Art of Monopoly: Standard Oil's Aggressive Expansion and Consolidation Tactics

"Competition is a sin." These infamous words, attributed to John D. Rockefeller, epitomized the ruthless business philosophy that would transform Standard Oil into history's most formidable monopoly. Through a combination of strategic genius and controversial tactics, Rockefeller orchestrated what became known as "The Cleveland Massacre," a dramatic consolidation of power that would forever change American industry.

In February 1872, Rockefeller launched his most audacious campaign yet. Through secret negotiations with the South Improvement Company, he secured preferential railroad rates that gave Standard Oil an insurmountable advantage. [32] The scheme was breathtaking in its scope – Standard Oil would receive not only substantial rebates on its own shipments but also "drawbacks" on its competitors' shipments. For every barrel of oil a rival company shipped, the railroad would pay Standard Oil a portion of the fee. [32]

The impact was devastating and immediate. Independent refiners found themselves paying up to 50% more in shipping costs than Standard Oil. Within three months, 22 of Cleveland's 26 refineries had either sold out to Standard Oil or shuttered their doors forever. [42] One by one, Rockefeller's agents visited his competitors, presenting them with stark choices – sell at Standard Oil's price or face certain ruin.

The case of Alexander, Scofield & Company illustrated the brutal efficiency of Rockefeller's tactics. When the company's owners initially refused to sell, Standard Oil's agents arranged for their oil shipments to be "delayed" by cooperative railroads. [39,42] Their barrels mysteriously disappeared en route to customers. Within weeks, facing financial collapse, they capitulated and sold to Standard Oil for a fraction of their company's worth.

In 1882, Rockefeller pioneered a new form of corporate organization – the trust. By exchanging their companies' stock for trust certificates, Standard Oil's partners created a centralized management structure that controlled 41 separate companies while technically keeping them independent. [39,32] This innovative legal structure became so successful that it inspired the term "antitrust" legislation.

The human cost of this consolidation was immense. Thousands of independent refiners, oil producers, and workers saw their livelihoods destroyed. In the oil regions of Pennsylvania, once-prosperous communities fell into economic depression. The era's newspapers were filled with stories of ruined businessmen, some of whom took their own lives rather than face bankruptcy. [39]

Yet Rockefeller viewed this consolidation as necessary progress, comparing it to the law of nature where "the American Beauty rose can be produced in its splendor and fragrance only by sacrificing the early buds that grow up around it." His methods, while brutal, introduced unprecedented efficiency to the oil industry. Standard Oil's integrated operations reduced the cost of kerosene from 58 cents to 8 cents per gallon, making artificial light affordable for millions of Americans. [38,32]

The legacy of Standard Oil's monopolistic practices continues to shape American business and regulation today. The Sherman Antitrust Act of 1890 was largely written in response to Standard Oil's dominance, establishing principles of competition that still govern American business. [40,41] When the Supreme Court finally ordered Standard Oil's dissolution in 1911, it created 34 independent companies, including the ancestors of modern-day ExxonMobil and Chevron. [32,42] Perhaps most importantly, the story of Standard Oil's rise and fall established an enduring tension in American capitalism between the efficiency of large-scale enterprise and the importance of market competition – a debate that continues to resonate in our discussions of modern tech giants and corporate consolidation.

The methods Rockefeller pioneered – vertical integration, strategic acquisition, and efficient scale – became templates for modern corporate organization. [38,32] Yet his tactics also sparked a progressive reform movement that fundamentally reshaped the relationship between government and business in American society. [42] The story of Standard Oil's monopolistic expansion remains a cautionary tale about the dangers of unchecked corporate power, while simultaneously demonstrating the transformative potential of industrial organization and efficiency. [43]

The Standard Oil Trust: Revolutionary Corporate Structure and Control

"The day of combination is here to stay. Individualism has gone, never to return." - John D. Rockefeller

On a cold January day in 1882, nine men gathered in the Standard Oil offices at 44 Broadway in New York City. Their task was unprecedented – the creation of the most sophisticated and powerful business organization the world had ever seen. [32,44,35] As they signed the trust agreement that would revolutionize American business, even these titans of industry could not have fully grasped how their actions would reshape corporate America forever.

The Standard Oil Trust represented a masterpiece of legal and financial engineering. By exchanging their shares in various oil companies for trust certificates, Rockefeller and his associates created a mechanism for centralized control while maintaining the appearance of independent operations. The trust would hold the stock of 41 companies, with the nine trustees wielding power over an empire that spanned the continent. [32,35]

The complexity of this new structure was illustrated by the meticulous documentation prepared for that January meeting. The trust agreement ran to over 47 pages, with each paragraph carefully crafted to navigate the legal restrictions of the time. [32,35] This was no mere business arrangement – it was the birth of modern corporate America.

The trust's impact on the oil industry was immediate and profound. Through this new structure, Standard Oil achieved unprecedented operational efficiency. The trust could coordinate production across multiple refineries, optimize transportation networks, and standardize product quality in ways that had been impossible under fragmented ownership. [37,45,35] The price of kerosene, the primary product of oil refining, brought affordable light to millions of American homes. [37,36]

Yet this efficiency came at a cost. The trust's power over the oil industry was nearly absolute. Through its control of refineries, pipelines, and transportation networks, Standard Oil could dictate terms to both producers and distributors. [37,45,35] Independent operators found themselves squeezed out of the market, unable to compete with the trust's integrated operations.

The human drama of this transformation played out in oil towns across America. In Titusville, Pennsylvania, where the American oil industry had begun, independent producers watched helplessly as the trust's power grew. The trust's agents would appear at struggling refineries, offering to buy them out at prices that reflected their weakened position. Those who refused often found themselves unable to ship their oil as railroad companies, influenced by secret rebate agreements with Standard Oil, suddenly had no cars available for independent shippers. [32,37,44]

The trust's dominance sparked intense public debate about the nature of corporate power in a democratic society. Critics saw it as a threat to American ideals of free enterprise and competition. Defenders argued that its efficiency and economies of scale benefited consumers through lower prices. [39,45] This tension between corporate efficiency and market competition would define American economic debates for generations to come.

The trust's innovative structure became a model for other industries. Soon, similar arrangements appeared in sugar, tobacco, and steel. The very term "antitrust" entered the American lexicon because of Standard Oil's example. When Congress passed the Sherman Antitrust Act in 1890, it was largely in response to the power of these new business combinations. [39,45]

The legacy of the Standard Oil Trust extends far beyond its eventual dissolution by the Supreme Court in 1911. [32,44] Its influence can be seen in modern corporate structures, antitrust legislation, and ongoing debates about market concentration and corporate power. The trust pioneered concepts of vertical integration, economies of scale, and professional management that remain central to business strategy today. [32,45,35]

Perhaps most significantly, the trust demonstrated both the potential and perils of concentrated economic power. As we grapple with questions about the role of large technology companies and corporate consolidation in our own time, the story of the Standard Oil Trust offers important lessons about the balance between efficiency and competition, innovation and regulation, private power and public good.

The parallels to modern America are striking. Just as the Standard Oil Trust used innovative legal structures to consolidate power, today's tech giants employ complex corporate arrangements to maintain market dominance. The debates about Standard Oil's control over essential infrastructure echo current discussions about platform monopolies and data control. [37,45,35] Even the trust's global reach and influence over American politics find modern parallels in discussions about corporate power and democratic governance.

Railroad Rebates and Business Ethics: The Controversial Path to Dominance

"The public be damned! I'm working for my stockholders." - William Henry Vanderbilt's infamous 1882 response to questions about railroad rebates

The morning sun cast long shadows through the windows of Standard Oil's Cleveland headquarters as John D. Rockefeller reviewed his latest railroad contracts. The year was 1871, and before him lay documents that would reshape American industry – secret agreements with the nation's largest railroads that would give his company unprecedented advantages over competitors. These weren't mere shipping contracts; they were weapons in his arsenal of industrial dominance.

The railroad rebate system that Rockefeller perfected was breathtaking in its scope and devastating in its impact. Through carefully negotiated agreements, Standard Oil received not only substantial discounts on its own shipments but also collected "drawbacks" – payments from the railroads based on the shipping fees paid by Rockefeller's competitors. [46,48] For every barrel of oil a rival company shipped, the railroad would secretly pay Standard Oil a portion of the fee. It was a system that essentially forced Rockefeller's competitors to subsidize their own destruction.

The human cost of these arrangements became painfully clear in the case of the Columbia Oil Company of Pittsburgh. In 1872, its owner arrived at his refinery to find his oil shipments indefinitely delayed by railroad companies bound by secret agreements with Standard Oil. His storage tanks overflowing and unable to ship his product to market, he faced the same choice confronting dozens of other independent refiners – sell to Standard Oil at a fraction of his company's worth or face certain bankruptcy. Within weeks, Columbia Oil became another asset in Rockefeller's growing empire.

The rebate system's power lay in its secrecy and complexity. Railroad companies, desperate for Standard Oil's guaranteed high-volume shipping, entered into elaborate agreements that were often hidden even from their own shareholders. [46,41] These arrangements became so intricate that by 1879, Standard Oil controlled not just oil refining but had effectively become the master of America's transportation networks. The company's power was such that it could dictate terms to the very railroads that had once held monopoly power over shipping rates.

The ethical implications of these practices sparked intense public debate. Critics saw them as a fundamental violation of fair competition, while defenders argued they simply reflected the natural advantages of scale and efficiency. [47] The reality was more complex – while rebates helped Standard Oil achieve unprecedented operational efficiency and lower consumer prices, they also created an uneven playing field that made true market competition impossible.

Public outrage over these practices eventually led to the Elkins Act of 1903, which prohibited discriminatory rebates and marked the beginning of federal regulation of railroad pricing. [48] Yet by then, Standard Oil's dominance was complete. The company controlled 90% of America's oil refining capacity, and Rockefeller had become the world's richest man through a system that redefined the boundaries of business ethics.

The legacy of railroad rebates extends far beyond their eventual prohibition. They demonstrated how control over vital infrastructure could be leveraged to build industrial empires, a lesson that resonates in today's debates about digital platforms and network effects. The public backlash against these practices helped establish the principle that certain business tactics, however profitable, could be deemed contrary to public interest – a concept that remains central to modern antitrust law. [33,46]

As we grapple with questions about market dominance in the digital age, the story of Standard Oil's railroad rebates offers striking parallels. Just as Rockefeller used control over transportation networks to build his monopoly, modern tech giants leverage control over digital infrastructure to maintain market dominance. The fundamental questions remain the same: How do we balance efficiency and competition? When does business innovation cross the line into anti-competitive behavior? What role should government play in regulating powerful corporate entities?

The era of railroad rebates may be long past, but its lessons about the intersection of business ethics, corporate power, and public interest continue to shape our understanding of market regulation and corporate responsibility. In many ways, the debates sparked by Rockefeller's controversial path to dominance remain as relevant today as they were in the Gilded Age.

The Sherman Antitrust Act and Standard Oil's Dissolution

"The power to regulate commerce... does not carry with it the power to destroy commerce." - Chief Justice Edward D. White, Standard Oil Co. of New Jersey v. United States, 1911

On a crisp May morning in 1911, the marble corridors of the Supreme Court echoed with footsteps as Chief Justice Edward D. White prepared to deliver one of the most consequential decisions in American business history. The fate of the world's largest corporation – and the future of American capitalism – hung in the balance. After years of litigation, the highest court in the land was about to rule on whether Standard Oil, the empire John D. Rockefeller had built over four decades, would survive or be dismantled.

The path to this historic moment began two decades earlier with the Sherman Antitrust Act of 1890. Named after Senator John Sherman of Ohio, the Act represented America's first attempt to address the growing power of industrial monopolies. Its language was sweeping: any contract, combination, or conspiracy that restrained trade was declared illegal. [49,51] Yet for years, the Act remained largely unenforced, a paper tiger that seemed to pose little threat to Standard Oil's dominance.

The tide began to turn in 1906 when President Theodore Roosevelt's administration filed suit against Standard Oil under the Sherman Act. The government's case was built on years of evidence, including the devastating exposé by journalist Ida Tarbell, whose 'history of the Standard Oil Company' had laid bare the company's predatory practices. [32,54] Tarbell's work, published in McClure's Magazine, had particular resonance – her own father had been one of the independent oilmen driven to ruin by Rockefeller's ruthless tactics.

In the Supreme Court chambers that May morning, Chief Justice White introduced a new concept into American law – the 'rule of reason.' Not all monopolies were inherently illegal, he declared, only those that had achieved their dominance through unreasonable methods. In Standard Oil's case, the evidence of such unreasonable practices was overwhelming. The company had systematically eliminated competition through railroad rebates, predatory pricing, and industrial espionage. [50,33] The Court's verdict was unanimous – Standard Oil must be dissolved. [49,51,54]

The breakup created 34 independent companies, including Standard Oil of New Jersey (later Exxon), Standard Oil of New York (later Mobil), Standard Oil of California (later Chevron), and Standard Oil of Indiana (later Amoco). In what seemed like cosmic irony, the dissolution actually increased Rockefeller's wealth. As the separate companies traded on the open market, the combined value of his stockholdings doubled, making him the richest man in the world. [32,52,53]

The human impact of this decision rippled across America. In the oil regions of Pennsylvania, independent producers who had lived under Standard Oil's shadow for decades celebrated their liberation.

In Cleveland, where Rockefeller had built his empire, workers at the various Standard Oil facilities faced an uncertain future as their company was carved into pieces. The breakup marked the end of an era – the age of unfettered industrial consolidation was over.

The legacy of the Standard Oil case continues to shape American business regulation today. The 'rule of reason' established by Chief Justice White remains a cornerstone of antitrust law, guiding courts as they grapple with modern monopolies in the digital age. [49,45] The parallels between Standard Oil's control of energy infrastructure and current debates about tech companies' dominance of digital platforms are striking. Just as Rockefeller's empire was built on controlling the flow of oil, today's tech giants derive their power from controlling the flow of information and data.

The dissolution of Standard Oil marked a crucial turning point in American capitalism – a recognition that while business success should be rewarded, unchecked corporate power poses risks to both economic freedom and democratic society. [53,54] As we continue to debate the role of government in regulating business, the lessons of Standard Oil's rise and fall remain remarkably relevant. The fundamental questions persist: How do we balance efficiency with competition? When does corporate size become dangerous to public interest? What limits should be placed on private economic power in a democratic society?

In many ways, the antitrust revolution that began with Standard Oil's breakup helped create the modern American economy – one that attempts to balance the benefits of large-scale enterprise with the importance of market competition. As we face similar challenges with today's tech giants, the story of Standard Oil's dissolution offers crucial lessons about the delicate balance between corporate power and public good.

Legacy of Standard Oil: Modern Oil Companies and Corporate Regulation

"The meek shall inherit the Earth, but not its mineral rights." - J. Paul Getty, reflecting on the oil industry's enduring power

In late 1911, as the Supreme Court's decision to break up Standard Oil reverberated through Wall Street, few could have predicted how this landmark ruling would reshape not just the oil industry, but the very fabric of American capitalism. The dissolution of Rockefeller's empire into 34 separate companies didn't diminish its collective power – instead, it seeded the ground for today's global energy giants and established principles of corporate regulation that continue to govern business practices. [42,32]

The immediate aftermath of the breakup revealed both the genius of the Court's decision and the resilience of Rockefeller's creation. The separate companies, freed from their parent organization, began competing and innovating in ways that transformed the industry. Rather than destroying Rockefeller's wealth, the breakup ironically doubled his fortune as the combined value of the separate companies' stocks soared.

The human drama of this transformation played out in oil towns across America. In Bayonne, New Jersey, where Standard Oil of New Jersey operated one of the world's largest refineries, workers witnessed their company's evolution from a local powerhouse into Exxon, a global energy giant. The refinery's transformation mirrored the industry's broader changes – from focusing primarily on kerosene for lighting to producing gasoline for the burgeoning automobile industry. [55,32]

The breakup's influence extended far beyond the oil industry. The Supreme Court's 'rule of reason' doctrine, established in the Standard Oil case, became the cornerstone of American antitrust law. This principle – that only unreasonable restraints of trade were illegal – provided a flexible framework for balancing business efficiency with market competition. [42] The case established precedents that would guide corporate regulation for generations, influencing everything from the breakup of AT&T to modern antitrust actions against tech giants. [42,56]

The legacy of Standard Oil's dissolution continues to shape contemporary debates about corporate power. Today's discussions about breaking up companies like Amazon, Google, or Facebook echo the arguments made during Standard Oil's case. The fundamental questions remain remarkably similar: How much market power is too much? When does corporate efficiency become harmful to competition? What role should government play in regulating business? [42,32]

The successor companies to Standard Oil have themselves become global titans, demonstrating the enduring power of Rockefeller's original vision. ExxonMobil, formed by the 1999 merger of two Standard Oil descendants, became one of the world's largest corporations. Chevron, BP (which acquired Standard Oil of Ohio), and other 'Baby Standards' dominate the global energy landscape, their combined influence arguably exceeding that of the original Standard Oil Trust. [55,58,59]

Yet these companies operate in a regulatory environment fundamentally shaped by their predecessor's dissolution. The antitrust framework established by the Standard Oil case created a distinctly American approach to corporate regulation – one that seeks to balance the benefits of large-scale enterprise with the importance of market competition. [42,56] This legacy is visible not just in oil industry regulation but in how we approach corporate power across all sectors of the economy.

The story of Standard Oil's legacy is ultimately one of unintended consequences. The breakup designed to limit corporate power instead demonstrated how regulation could foster both competition and growth. [56,57] As we face similar challenges with today's tech giants and global corporations, the lessons of Standard Oil's dissolution remain surprisingly relevant. The balance between innovation and regulation, between corporate efficiency and market competition, continues to shape our economic landscape, much as it did in the aftermath of that momentous Supreme Court decision over a century ago.

In many ways, modern American capitalism was forged in the crucible of Standard Oil's breakup. The principles established then – about the limits of corporate power, the importance of market competition, and the role of government oversight – continue to influence how we think about business and regulation today. [42,32] As we grapple with questions of corporate influence in the digital age, the echoes of Standard Oil's legacy remind us that the fundamental challenges of balancing private power with public good remain as relevant as ever .As the 19th century drew to a close, Standard Oil's dominance over American industry stood as a testament to both the transformative potential and the darker implications of unfettered capitalism. John D. Rockefeller's methodical rise from bookkeeper to billionaire had fundamentally reshaped not just the oil industry, but the very nature of American business. His legacy would echo through the corridors of corporate America for generations to come.

The story of Standard Oil is, in many ways, the story of modern American capitalism itself. Through innovation and ruthless efficiency, Rockefeller created an organization of unprecedented scale and sophistication. The price of kerosene fell from 58 cents to 8 cents per gallon, bringing affordable light to millions of American homes. Yet this progress came at a devastating human cost, as thousands of independent refiners and oil producers saw their livelihoods destroyed by Standard Oil's relentless expansion.

The methods Rockefeller pioneered – vertical integration, strategic acquisition, professional management – became templates for corporate organization that persist to this day. His trust structure, though eventually outlawed, laid the groundwork for modern corporate organization. Even the antitrust laws created to check Standard Oil's power continue to shape business regulation in our own time.

Perhaps most significantly, Standard Oil's story illuminates the eternal tension between efficiency and competition, between private power and public good. The questions raised by Rockefeller's monopoly remain startlingly relevant in our modern digital age. As we grapple with the power of tech giants and debate the role of corporate influence in democracy, the echoes of the Gilded Age remind us that the fundamental challenges of balancing innovation with regulation, progress with fairness, continue to shape our economic landscape.

Just as the dissolution of Standard Oil in 1911 didn't diminish its collective power but rather seeded the ground for today's global energy giants, the principles established during its reign – about the limits of corporate power, the importance of market competition, and the role of government oversight – continue to influence how we think about business and regulation today. In the end, Rockefeller's legacy serves as both inspiration and warning, a reminder of capitalism's capacity for both creation and destruction, for both progress and exploitation.

As we face our own era's challenges of corporate consolidation and technological disruption, the lessons of Standard Oil's rise and fall remain as relevant as ever. The fundamental questions persist: How do we balance efficiency with competition? When does corporate size become dangerous to public interest? What limits should be placed on private economic power in a democratic society? In seeking answers to these questions, we would do well to remember both the triumphs and the transgressions of John D. Rockefeller's remarkable empire.

Chapter Three

Steel and Soul: Andrew Carnegie's Industrial Revolution and the Gospel of Wealth

The piercing whistle of the steel mill cut through the smoky air of Pittsburgh in 1875, as Andrew Carnegie stood before his first blast furnace at the Edgar Thomson Steel Works, watching liquid steel pour like golden rivers into waiting molds. The forty-year-old industrialist, who had arrived in America as a penniless immigrant just three decades earlier, was about to revolutionize the steel industry through technological innovation and vertical integration, forever changing both American industry and philanthropy. "Man must have an idol – the amassing of wealth is one of the worst species of idolatry." - Andrew Carnegie, 1889

The transformation of this immigrant boy into America's foremost steel magnate would become one of the most compelling narratives of the Gilded Age, embodying both the promise and paradox of American capitalism. Through relentless innovation and ruthless efficiency, Carnegie built an industrial empire that would quite literally provide the backbone of America's growth – the steel for its railroads, bridges, and skyscrapers. Yet his path to unprecedented wealth was paved with controversy and human cost, nowhere more evident than in the tragic events that would unfold at Homestead.

Carnegie's story was uniquely American – a tale of reinvention and relentless ambition. Rising from work as a bobbin boy in a cotton factory to become the richest man in the world, he pioneered revolutionary methods in steel production while simultaneously developing a complex philosophy about wealth and social responsibility. His implementation of the Bessemer process at the Edgar Thomson Works revolutionized steel manufacturing, drastically reducing costs while increasing output exponentially. This technological leap, combined with his vertical integration strategy – controlling everything from raw materials to transportation – created an unprecedented industrial machine.

However, the human cost of this efficiency would come to a head in the summer of 1892 at Carnegie's Homestead Steel Works. While Carnegie retreated to his Scottish castle, Skibo, his lieutenant Henry Clay Frick confronted the Amalgamated Association of Iron and Steel Workers with draconian wage cuts and union-breaking tactics. The resulting conflict would become one of the most violent labor disputes in American history, forever tainting Carnegie's reputation and accelerating his transition from industrialist to philanthropist.

In July 1892, as tensions reached their breaking point, Frick called in hundreds of Pinkerton agents to protect the mill and break the strike. The arrival of these armed men sparked a fierce battle along the Monongahela River. Workers and townspeople, armed with rifles and cannons, engaged in a day-long firefight with the Pinkertons. The bloody confrontation left ten dead and dozens wounded. Eventually, the Pennsylvania state militia restored order, but the union was broken, and with it, the spirit of organized labor in the steel industry for decades to come.

For Carnegie, who had built his empire through a combination of technological innovation and labor exploitation, the Homestead Strike marked a turning point. Though his mills continued to generate enormous profits with non-union labor, the violence at Homestead haunted him. This crisis of conscience led him to pen his famous essay "The Gospel of Wealth," which argued that the rich had a moral obligation to use their money to improve society. Carnegie would spend the remainder of his life giving away his fortune, establishing thousands of public libraries, funding educational institutions, and supporting the arts.

The Carnegie legacy exemplifies the complex dualities of the Gilded Age – extreme wealth alongside grinding poverty, technological progress alongside human exploitation, and ultimately, ruthless business practices alongside unprecedented philanthropy. His story raises questions that remain relevant today about the nature of capitalism, the responsibilities of wealth, and the true cost of progress in human terms. As modern debates rage about income inequality, workers' rights, and corporate responsibility, the echoes of Homestead and Carnegie's subsequent transformation continue to resonate, reminding us that the challenges of balancing profit and social good are as relevant now as they were in the Gilded Age.

The Bessemer Revolution: Carnegie's Technological Innovation in Steel Production

"The man who dies thus rich dies disgraced," Carnegie famously declared, but it was his mastery of the Bessemer process that first allowed him to amass the fortune he would later give away. On a foggy morning in 1872, Carnegie stood in awe before the massive Bessemer converters at the Cleveland Rolling Mills, watching as streams of white-hot air transformed molten pig iron into high-quality steel in mere minutes. [62,64,66] This revolutionary process would soon become the cornerstone of his industrial empire.

The Bessemer process, developed by English inventor Sir Henry Bessemer in 1856, represented the first inexpensive method for mass-producing steel. [62,64,66] As Carnegie later wrote in his autobiography, 'The Bessemer process of steel manufacture gave us the rails which made modern transportation possible.' The impact was immediate and dramatic – steel that once cost £50-60 per ton could now be produced for a mere £6-7, [64] transforming the economics of industrial production.

At the Edgar Thomson Works, completed in 1873 near Pittsburgh, Carnegie implemented the Bessemer process on an unprecedented scale. [60,63,65] The massive facility, named after the president of the Pennsylvania Railroad, became a testament to Carnegie's vision of industrial efficiency. The sight was awe-inspiring – massive converters tilting and roaring as they spewed flames and sparks, transforming raw iron into steel through the simple yet ingenious process of blowing air through the molten metal to remove impurities. [62,64,66]

Carnegie's genius lay not just in adopting the technology, but in relentlessly improving it. He hired the finest technical minds, including Captain William Jones, whose innovations at Edgar Thomson Works helped reduce production costs from $56 per ton to just $11.50 by 1900. [63] The plant operated around the clock, with three shifts of workers manning the converters in a carefully choreographed industrial ballet that produced more steel than any facility in the world.

The human cost of this efficiency was stark. Workers endured grueling twelve-hour shifts in dangerous conditions, where temperatures could exceed 130 degrees Fahrenheit. [61,65] As molten metal splashed and machinery roared, men risked their lives daily for wages that barely supported their families. Yet Carnegie's innovations were reshaping America itself. The steel pouring from his mills would soon rise in New York's first skyscrapers, span the nation's great rivers as bridges, and connect cities through a vast network of steel rails. [64,66]

Through vertical integration, Carnegie controlled every aspect of production – from the iron ore mines of Lake Superior to the coal fields of Pennsylvania, from the limestone quarries to the railroad lines that transported materials. [60,63] This strategic mastery allowed him to weather economic downturns that destroyed his competitors, while continuously driving down costs through economies of scale.

By 1900, Carnegie Steel was producing more steel than all of Britain combined. The United States had emerged as the world's leading industrial power, with an annual steel output of 10 million metric tons.

[65] The Bessemer revolution had transformed not just an industry, but a nation. Cities rose higher, bridges spanned wider, and railroads stretched further than ever before possible. [62,64,66]

The legacy of Carnegie's technological innovation extends far beyond the Gilded Age. Today's skyscrapers, bridges, and infrastructure still rely on the basic principles of mass steel production pioneered in those roaring Pittsburgh mills. [64,66] The modern American industrial economy, with its emphasis on vertical integration, economies of scale, and continuous technological improvement, bears the unmistakable imprint of Carnegie's methods. [60,63]

Perhaps most significantly, the wealth generated through these innovations – while built upon worker exploitation [61,65] – ultimately funded libraries, universities, and cultural institutions that continue to enrich American society. The story of the Bessemer revolution thus embodies both the tremendous creative and destructive forces of American industrialization, forces that continue to shape our nation's economic and social landscape today.

Vertical Integration and Cost Accounting: The Carnegie System of Business Management

"Watch the costs and the profits will take care of themselves." These words, spoken by Andrew Carnegie to his managers, embodied the revolutionary business system he created – one that would transform not just the steel industry, but the very nature of American capitalism.

On a cold December morning in 1872, Carnegie sat in his office at the Union Iron Mills, poring over detailed cost sheets that tracked every penny spent in his operations. The previous day's production figures, material costs, and labor expenses were meticulously documented in columns of precise numbers. [67,69] This obsession with data and efficiency would become the cornerstone of his empire. Unlike his competitors, who often operated on rough estimates and gut feelings, Carnegie demanded exact figures for everything – from the cost of ore at the mines to the final price of each steel rail. [69]

Carnegie's system of vertical integration was breathtaking in its scope and ambition. By 1897, he controlled not just steel mills but a vast network of resources and transportation that included iron ore deposits in Lake Superior, coal fields in Pennsylvania, a fleet of steamships on the Great Lakes, and miles of railroad track. [69] This comprehensive control allowed him to slash costs at every stage of production, creating an efficiency that his competitors couldn't match. [69,68]

The heart of Carnegie's business genius lay in his revolutionary cost accounting system. Every day, detailed reports from each department arrived on managers' desks before noon, showing the previous day's expenses down to the fraction of a penny per ton of steel produced. [67,69] These 'cost sheets' became famous throughout the industry, striking fear into competitors who couldn't understand how Carnegie consistently underbid them while maintaining profits. [69]

In 1880, during a particularly fierce price war, Carnegie demonstrated the power of his system. When competitors were losing money on steel rails priced at $50 per ton, Carnegie's detailed cost sheets showed he could still profit at $40. [69] His mills' efficiency, combined with the cost savings from vertical integration, allowed him to weather market downturns that bankrupted other manufacturers. [69,68]

Carnegie's management innovations extended beyond mere numbers. He pioneered what became known as the 'Carnegie Partnership System,' promoting young, talented managers and giving them ownership stakes in the business. [67,69] Charles Schwab, who started as a stake-driver's assistant, rose to become president of Carnegie Steel by age thirty-five, exemplifying Carnegie's merit-based approach to management. [67]

However, this relentless pursuit of efficiency had its human costs. Workers endured grueling conditions as Carnegie's cost accounting system demanded ever-increasing productivity. [69] Every minute of downtime was tracked, every ounce of material waste noted. The pressure to reduce costs often translated into wage cuts and speedups, contributing to the labor tensions that would eventually explode at Homestead.

Yet Carnegie's system revolutionized American industry. His integration of raw material sources, transportation networks, and production facilities created a model that would be emulated by corporations throughout the 20th century. [69] Companies like Ford Motor Company and Standard Oil would adopt similar vertical integration strategies, while Carnegie's cost accounting methods became standard practice in modern business management. [15,61]

The legacy of Carnegie's business system extends far beyond the Gilded Age. Today's emphasis on data-driven decision making, supply chain integration, and operational efficiency can be traced back to the innovations he introduced. [69] Modern corporations still struggle with the same fundamental challenge he faced: balancing operational efficiency with human costs. As we grapple with questions of corporate responsibility, worker rights, and sustainable business practices, the lessons and contradictions of Carnegie's system remain remarkably relevant.

In our current age of global supply chains and big data analytics, Carnegie's obsession with vertical integration and precise cost accounting seems remarkably prescient. [69] His system demonstrated both the tremendous potential and the human challenges of industrial efficiency – a tension that continues to define American capitalism in the 21st century.

The Homestead Strike of 1892: Labor Relations and Industrial Violence

"There was a time when the power of corporations was checked by public sentiment. That day seems to have passed." - Hugh O'Donnell, strike leader at Homestead, 1892

On the sweltering morning of July 6, 1892, the usually bustling town of Homestead, Pennsylvania, awoke to an eerie silence. The massive steel mills that dominated the landscape stood quiet, their smokestacks cold for the first time in years. But the calm was deceptive. Along the banks of the Monongahela River, thousands of steelworkers and their families gathered in the pre-dawn darkness, watching intently for any sign of movement on the water's surface. They knew what was coming. [70,72]

In the luxurious confines of his Scottish castle, Andrew Carnegie was deliberately absent, having delegated the handling of the impending crisis to his lieutenant, Henry Clay Frick. [70,74,76] While Carnegie enjoyed the comforts of his estate, Frick had spent weeks preparing for this confrontation, constructing a fortress-like wall around the mill topped with barbed wire and sniper posts – a barrier that workers mockingly dubbed "Fort Frick." [70,73,74]

The tension had been building for months. When the existing labor contract approached expiration, Frick had demanded massive wage cuts and refused to negotiate with the Amalgamated Association of Iron and Steel Workers. [70,72,75] His ultimate goal was clear – to break the union's power once and for all. The workers, many of whom had spent decades building Carnegie's empire, faced an impossible choice: accept poverty wages or fight.

At dawn, the first signs of trouble appeared – two barges being towed upriver, laden with hundreds of armed Pinkerton agents hired by Frick to seize control of the mill. What followed was one of the bloodiest labor conflicts in American history. As the Pinkertons attempted to land, gunfire erupted from both sides. The battle raged for twelve hours, leaving ten men dead – seven workers and three Pinkerton agents – and dozens more wounded. [70,71,72]

The violence shocked the nation. Newspapers carried dramatic accounts of the battle, with some comparing it to the civil war battles of recent memory. The striking workers initially gained control of the town, forcing the Pinkertons to surrender and retreat under a gauntlet of angry townspeople. But their victory would be short-lived.

Governor Robert Pattison soon deployed 8,500 National Guard troops to Homestead, effectively placing the town under martial law. [70,72,76] The mill reopened with replacement workers, protected by rows of bayonets. Union leaders faced arrest and imprisonment. By November, with their resources exhausted and their spirits broken, the workers began returning to their jobs under Frick's harsh terms – longer hours, lower wages, and no union representation. [72,76]

The human cost was staggering. Families who had lived comfortably on union wages now struggled to survive. Children left school to work in factories. The community's social fabric, built over generations, began to unravel. Meanwhile, Carnegie's profits soared as labor costs plummeted. The contrast between his public philanthropy and private brutality became impossible to ignore. [70,74,76]

The aftermath of Homestead reshaped American labor relations for decades to come. The defeat of one of the nation's strongest unions sent a chilling message to organized labor everywhere. Companies across the country adopted Carnegie's tactics, using private armies and government troops to break strikes and unions. The era of the "robber barons" reached its violent apex, as the power of industrial capitalism seemed unstoppable. [71,72,76]

Yet Homestead's legacy extends far beyond its immediate aftermath. The strike became a powerful symbol of the struggle between labor and capital, inspiring generations of workers' rights advocates. The violence at Homestead contributed to growing public awareness of industrial working conditions and eventually helped spark Progressive Era reforms. The images of armed Pinkertons attacking American workers raised crucial questions about corporate power and private armies – questions that remain relevant in discussions of private security contractors today. [70,72,76]

Perhaps most significantly, Homestead exposed the fundamental contradictions of the Gilded Age – how the enormous wealth generated by American industry came at a devastating human cost. The strike revealed the stark reality behind Carnegie's Gospel of Wealth philosophy, showing how his charitable giving was built upon the broken bodies and spirits of his workers. [70,74,76] This tension between corporate profit and human dignity continues to resonate in modern debates about income inequality, workers' rights, and corporate responsibility.

Today, as we grapple with questions of labor rights, income inequality, and the power of corporations in American society, the echoes of Homestead still reverberate. The strike's central questions – about the balance of power between workers and employers, the role of government in labor disputes, and the social responsibilities of wealth – remain as relevant now as they were in 1892. [70,72,76] The ghosts of Homestead still haunt our national conversation about work, wealth, and justice in America.

The Gospel of Wealth: Carnegie's Philosophy of Philanthropic Responsibility

"The problem of our age is the proper administration of wealth, so that the ties of brotherhood may still bind together the rich and poor in harmonious relationship." - Andrew Carnegie, 1889

On a crisp autumn morning in 1889, Andrew Carnegie sat in his study at his Fifth Avenue mansion, penning what would become one of the most influential essays in American history. The contrast between his surroundings – the mahogany-paneled walls, Persian carpets, and gilt-framed paintings – and the subject of his writing was not lost on him. His article for the North American Review, soon to be known as "The Gospel of Wealth," would challenge America's wealthy elite to fundamentally rethink their relationship with their fortunes.

Carnegie's philosophy emerged from his own remarkable journey from poverty to unprecedented wealth. Having experienced both grinding poverty in Scotland and enormous success in America, he developed a unique perspective on wealth's purpose and responsibilities. His essay argued that the concentration of wealth in the hands of the few was both inevitable and beneficial to society – provided those few understood their moral obligation to use that wealth for the greater good. [77,81]

The timing of Carnegie's manifesto was deliberate. The previous year, he had watched as New York's wealthy paraded their fortunes at the infamous Bradley-Martin Ball, where socialites dressed as Marie Antoinette and Louis XVI, seemingly oblivious to the bitter irony of emulating French aristocrats who had met their end at the guillotine. The extravaganza had cost $400,000 (equivalent to over $12 million today) while working families struggled to survive on dollars a day.

This display of conspicuous consumption horrified Carnegie, who saw it as a dangerous provocation of class tensions.

"The man who dies thus rich, dies disgraced," Carnegie declared in his essay, challenging the prevailing attitudes of his fellow millionaires. [80,81] He outlined three options for wealth: Leaving it to family members, bequeathing it for public purposes after death, or administering it during one's lifetime. The first he condemned as harmful to both heirs and society, the second he dismissed as cowardly, leaving only the third as truly noble and worthy. [77,81]

Carnegie's philosophy translated into unprecedented charitable giving. By 1911, he had funded the construction of 2,509 libraries across the English-speaking world, including 1,679 in the United States alone. [78,80] Each library represented a chance for self-improvement, a ladder of opportunity for ambitious workers like his younger self. He established universities, research institutions, and foundations that continue to shape American intellectual and cultural life today. [78,82]

Yet Carnegie's philanthropy was not without its critics. Labor leaders pointed out the irony of building libraries with money squeezed from underpaid workers. Following the Homestead Strike, one union newspaper bitterly observed that Carnegie was "trying to ease his conscience by giving away money that he had stolen from the steel workers." The contrast between his charitable giving and his business practices highlighted the complex moral calculations of Gilded Age philanthropy. [79,65]

The impact of Carnegie's "Gospel of Wealth" extended far beyond his own giving. John D. Rockefeller, who had previously given mainly to Baptist causes, began to approach philanthropy more systematically, establishing the Rockefeller Foundation in 1913. Henry Clay Frick, Carnegie's former partner, would leave his magnificent art collection and mansion to New York City as a public museum. The essay helped establish a new American tradition of philanthropic responsibility among the wealthy. [80]

Today, Carnegie's philosophy continues to influence modern philanthropy. The Giving Pledge, created by Bill Gates and Warren Buffett, echoes Carnegie's call for the wealthy to give away the majority of their fortunes. [80] Major foundations still struggle with the same questions Carnegie raised about how to give effectively rather than merely generously. His emphasis on creating opportunities for self-improvement rather than mere charity remains a guiding principle for many philanthropists. [77,78,81]

The tension Carnegie identified between private wealth and public good remains at the heart of American debates about inequality and social responsibility. As modern billionaires face increasing scrutiny over their wealth and influence, Carnegie's "Gospel of Wealth" offers both inspiration and warning – a reminder that with great fortune comes great responsibility, and that the ultimate value of wealth lies not in its accumulation but in its wise distribution for the benefit of all. [79,82]

Carnegie Libraries: Transforming Public Education and Access to Knowledge

"The man who dies rich, dies disgraced." These words, spoken by Andrew Carnegie in 1889, took physical form in thousands of red-brick buildings that would transform American society. On a bright September morning in 1895, Carnegie stood before the newly completed Pittsburgh public library, his first major library gift in America. The magnificent structure, with its marble stairs and vaulted reading room, represented more than just a building – it was the embodiment of his belief that knowledge could lift anyone from poverty to prosperity, just as it had done for him.

The story of Carnegie's libraries began in his youth, in the small Scottish town of Dunfermline, where as a poor weaver's son he had been granted access to a private library by Colonel James Anderson. [84,86] Years later, Carnegie would write in his autobiography that those precious books had opened the world to him. This personal experience shaped his conviction that free access to knowledge was the greatest gift one could give to a community.

By 1919, Carnegie had funded 2,509 libraries worldwide, with 1,689 of them spread across the American landscape. [83,84] Each library represented a carefully calculated investment in human potential. The 'Carnegie Formula' required communities to demonstrate their commitment by providing the land and pledging annual operating funds equal to 10% of his construction grant. [83,86] This was not charity, he insisted, but rather an investment in self-reliance.

In Homestead, Pennsylvania, the irony of Carnegie's philanthropy was particularly stark. Just three years after the bloody strike at his steel mill, Carnegie offered the town $300,000 for a library. [82,65] Many workers initially opposed accepting the gift, with one union leader declaring, 'We don't want your charity at the expense of our brothers' lives.' Yet the library was eventually built, and despite its controversial origins, became a center of learning for generations of steelworkers' children.

The libraries themselves were architectural marvels, designed to inspire as much as educate. Each featured high ceilings, large windows for natural light, and open stacks – a revolutionary concept at the time. [83] The words 'FREE TO ALL' were often carved above their entrances, a radical declaration in an age of private clubs and restricted access. Inside, working-class immigrants sat alongside middle-class readers, creating one of America's first truly democratic spaces.

The impact of these libraries was profound and immediate. In 1900, before the great wave of Carnegie libraries, only about 900 public libraries existed in the United States. By 1923, thanks largely to Carnegie's initiative, that number had swelled to over 3,500. [83] The libraries became sanctuaries of self-improvement, where factory workers could study technical manuals, immigrants could learn English, and children could discover worlds beyond their neighborhoods. [86]

One of the most remarkable aspects of Carnegie's library program was its timing. As America underwent rapid industrialization and waves of immigration, these libraries provided crucial infrastructure for social mobility and cultural assimilation. [86] They were particularly transformative for women, offering respectable employment as librarians and safe spaces for independent study at a time when both were rare.

The legacy of Carnegie libraries extends far beyond their brick and mortar foundations. They established the model for modern public libraries – open stacks, children's sections, community meeting spaces, and the fundamental principle that knowledge should be freely accessible to all. [83] Today, about 770 of the original Carnegie libraries still serve their communities, while others have been repurposed as museums, community centers, and civic spaces.

Perhaps most significantly, Carnegie's library initiative helped establish the modern concept of strategic philanthropy. [84,85] His insistence on community matching funds, sustainable operations, and measurable outcomes created a template for philanthropic giving that continues to influence major foundations today. When Bill Gates cites Carnegie as an inspiration for his own charitable work, he's acknowledging not just the scale of Carnegie's giving, but the systematic approach behind it.

In our current age of digital disruption and growing inequality, Carnegie's libraries remind us that access to knowledge remains a powerful force for social mobility. As we grapple with questions of educational equity and the digital divide, the Carnegie library model – with its emphasis on free access, community investment, and the transformative power of learning – offers enduring lessons for addressing modern challenges. [86] The story of these libraries stands as testament to how strategic philanthropy, even when born from complex motivations, can create lasting positive change in society.

Legacy of Steel: Carnegie's Impact on American Industry and Philanthropy

"The man who dies rich, dies disgraced." These words, perhaps Carnegie's most famous declaration, echoed through the marble halls of his Fifth Avenue mansion in 1901 as he prepared to sell Carnegie Steel to J.P. Morgan for $480 million (equivalent to over $15 billion today). Standing at his office window, watching the steady stream of carriages along Fifth Avenue, Carnegie contemplated the transformation his steel empire had wrought on the American landscape – and the transformation he still hoped to achieve through its sale.

The impact of Carnegie's industrial innovations reshaped America in ways that remain visible today. By introducing the Bessemer process and implementing vertical integration, Carnegie had revolutionized steel production, driving prices down from $56 per ton to just $ 11.50. [82,87] This dramatic cost reduction made possible the soaring skyscrapers that would define the modern American cityscape. The steel that poured from his mills quite literally built the nation – from the Brooklyn Bridge to the railroads that spanned the continent. [87,89]

The scale of Carnegie's influence on American industry cannot be overstated. By 1900, his operations were producing more steel than all of Britain combined,[90] cementing America's position as the world's leading industrial power. The formation of U.S. Steel in 1901, which absorbed Carnegie Steel under J.P. Morgan's leadership, became the world's first billion-dollar corporation [61,89] – a watershed moment in business history that established patterns of corporate consolidation that would define 20th-century capitalism.

Yet Carnegie's most profound legacy lay not in the steel mills that had made him the world's richest man, but in how he chose to dispose of that fortune. His systematic approach to philanthropy – carefully structured to promote education, scientific research, and cultural advancement – established new paradigms for charitable giving that continue to influence modern philanthropists. [78,88] By 1919, he had funded 2,509 libraries worldwide, with 1,679 of them spread across America, dramatically expanding public access to knowledge. [80,78]

The Carnegie Institution for Science, founded in 1902, exemplified his commitment to advancing human knowledge. Rather than simply distributing wealth, Carnegie sought to create self-sustaining institutions that would continue generating benefits long after his death. [80,88] The Carnegie Endowment for International Peace, established in 1910 with a $10 million endowment, reflected his growing concern with global stability and cooperation. [80,88,78]

However, Carnegie's legacy remains complex and sometimes contradictory. The same man who wrote eloquently about workers' rights had overseen the brutal suppression of the Homestead Strike. [87,90] His libraries were built with profits squeezed from workers who could barely afford to feed their families. Yet even his harshest critics acknowledged the lasting impact of his philanthropic vision.

Today, Carnegie's influence resonates through institutions that continue to shape American society. The Carnegie Corporation of New York remains a powerful force in education and social reform. Carnegie Mellon University stands as a leading research institution. [80,88] The thousands of Carnegie libraries that still dot the American landscape continue to provide free access to knowledge for millions. [80,78]

Modern philanthropists like Bill Gates and Warren Buffett explicitly cite Carnegie's example in their own charitable giving. The Giving Pledge, which encourages billionaires to give away the majority of their wealth, echoes Carnegie's Gospel of Wealth. [78,88] Even the ongoing debates about wealth inequality, corporate responsibility, and the role of private philanthropy in public life trace their roots to questions Carnegie first grappled with over a century ago.

The story of Carnegie's legacy illuminates both the transformative potential and moral complexities of concentrated wealth. His life's work – both in industry and philanthropy – helped establish patterns of American capitalism and charitable giving that persist to this day. [61,87,90] As we continue to debate questions of economic inequality, corporate power, and social responsibility, Carnegie's complex legacy offers both inspiration and warning – a reminder that with great wealth comes great responsibility, and that true success lies not in the accumulation of riches, but in their wise distribution for the benefit of all. [82,78] As the sun set over Carnegie's empire of steel and philanthropy, the contradictions of the Gilded Age were cast in sharp relief. The transformation of a poor Scottish immigrant into America's foremost steel magnate embodied both the promise and paradox of

American capitalism – a tale of unprecedented innovation and wealth creation intertwined with human cost and moral complexity.

The story of Carnegie's steel empire reflects the broader themes that defined the Gilded Age. Through technological innovation like the Bessemer process and revolutionary management techniques, he built an industrial machine that literally constructed modern America. His vertical integration strategies and cost accounting systems created templates for corporate organization that would influence American business for generations to come. Yet the human toll of this efficiency was starkly revealed in the bloody confrontation at Homestead, where the struggle between capital and labor erupted into violence that would reshape American labor relations for decades.

Perhaps Carnegie's most enduring legacy lies not in the steel mills that made him the world's richest man, but in how he chose to dispose of that fortune. His Gospel of Wealth philosophy, which argued that the wealthy had a moral obligation to use their money for the betterment of society, established new paradigms for charitable giving that continue to influence modern philanthropy. The thousands of libraries he built across America dramatically expanded public access to knowledge and created a model for strategic philanthropy that resonates in the work of modern philanthropists like Bill Gates and Warren Buffett.

The tensions embodied in Carnegie's story – between profit and human dignity, between private wealth and public good – continue to define American capitalism. As we grapple with questions of income inequality, workers' rights, and corporate responsibility in our own time, the lessons of Carnegie's era remain startlingly relevant. His complex legacy serves as both inspiration and warning – a reminder that the greatest challenge facing any society is not merely the creation of wealth but ensuring that its benefits extend beyond the few to enrich the lives of all.

In the end, Carnegie's story illuminates the fundamental dualities of the Gilded Age – extreme wealth alongside grinding poverty, technological progress alongside human exploitation, and ultimately, ruthless business practices alongside unprecedented philanthropy. As modern debates rage about economic inequality, workers' rights, and the responsibilities of wealth, the echoes of Carnegie's era continue to resonate, reminding us that the challenges of balancing profit and social good remain as pressing today as they were in the age of steel.

Chapter Four

Banking Titans: J.P. Morgan and the Power of Wall Street

On a tense autumn morning in 1907, J.P. Morgan sat in his mahogany-paneled library on Madison Avenue, summoning New York's leading bankers to prevent a financial collapse that threatened to destroy the nation's economy. The sixty-nine-year-old financier, whose very presence could calm markets, was about to orchestrate one of the most remarkable private bailouts in American history, demonstrating both the extraordinary power of one man and the dangerous fragility of an unregulated banking system. "Money is the most important thing in the world," Morgan once declared, a statement that seemed to encapsulate both his philosophy and the era he dominated. His commanding presence in that library was about to demonstrate just how true those words had become in America's emerging industrial economy.

As the nation's preeminent financier, Morgan wielded unprecedented power over America's financial markets. His influence extended far beyond traditional banking – he restructured railroads, consolidated industries, and effectively served as America's central bank before the Federal Reserve existed. The very architecture of his library, with its imposing Renaissance-style façade and rich mahogany interiors, testified to both his immense wealth and his cultural aspirations. This was where he housed not just financial deals but also his world-renowned art collection, a testament to how America's financial titans sought to transform their monetary power into cultural capital.

The events of 1907 would prove to be Morgan's finest hour, revealing both the extraordinary reach of private banking power and its inherent dangers. When the Knickerbocker Trust Company failed in October, triggering a series of bank runs, Morgan transformed his library into a command center for saving the American economy. His methods were as forceful as they were effective. In one remarkable episode, he locked New York's leading bankers in his library overnight, refusing to let them leave until they committed to a $25 million rescue fund for weaker institutions. "This stops right here," Morgan thundered at the assembled financiers, demonstrating why his contemporaries called him "Jupiter" for his Olympian authority.

As trust companies faltered and stock prices plummeted, Morgan orchestrated a series of interventions that ultimately stabilized the market. He personally examined the books of troubled banks, decided which would receive rescue funds, and committed millions of his own money to restore confidence. When President Theodore Roosevelt asked what Morgan could do to save the situation, his response was characteristically direct: "I will do what I can." It was a promise that carried more weight than any government guarantee in those days before federal banking regulation.

The drama that unfolded in Morgan's library during those tense autumn days would have lasting implications for American finance. While Morgan's decisive action had saved the economy, the crisis exposed the dangers of having the nation's financial stability depend on the judgment and resources of a single private banker, no matter how capable. This realization would eventually lead to the creation of the Federal Reserve System in 1913, marking the beginning of modern American banking regulation.

Yet even as Morgan helped usher in this more regulated era of American capitalism, he remained a figure of both admiration and fear. His power to calm markets with his mere presence earned him the nickname "Old Jupiter," while his authority to decide the fate of corporations and banks led critics to accuse him of having too much control over the nation's economy. The debate over his legacy – whether he was a necessary stabilizing force or a dangerous concentration of private power – would shape discussions about financial regulation for generations to come.

Morgan's story epitomizes the complex inheritance of the Gilded Age: a time when private individuals wielded extraordinary power over public welfare, when financial innovation walked hand in hand with monopolistic control, and when the foundations of modern American capitalism were laid in both their productive and problematic aspects. The lessons learned from his handling of the 1907 crisis – about the need for institutional oversight, the dangers of concentrated financial power, and the delicate balance between private initiative and public interest – remain relevant in today's discussions of financial regulation and economic stability.

The Rise of Modern Banking: Morgan's Early Years and Innovation in Finance

"The first thing is character. Money cannot buy it... A man I do not trust could not get money from me on all the bonds in Christendom." - J.P. Morgan

On a brisk autumn morning in 1857, a young J.P. Morgan stepped onto the cobblestone streets of London, his father's words echoing in his ears: "Remember, the Morgan name means something." At just twenty years old, Morgan was beginning his apprenticeship at Peabody & Company, one of London's most prestigious merchant banks. [91,93] This moment would mark the beginning of a career that would revolutionize American banking and reshape the nation's economy.

The contrast between Morgan's privileged position and the common banker of his day was stark. While most financial workers toiled in cramped counting houses, Morgan learned his trade in the elegant offices of George Peabody, surrounded by mahogany furniture and Persian carpets. Yet it was here that Morgan developed his most important principle: character was the foundation of credit. He would later famously testify before Congress that loans were made based on a man's character, not just his collateral. [93,94]

Morgan's early years in banking coincided with a transformative period in American finance. The Civil War had created unprecedented demands for capital, and the rapid industrialization that followed required new financial instruments and institutions. Morgan recognized these changes with remarkable prescience. Working first at Duncan, Sherman & Co. in New York, he began developing innovative methods for financing America's expanding railroads, a sector that would become crucial to his later success. [91]

In 1871, Morgan partnered with Anthony Drexel to form Drexel, Morgan & Co., establishing himself as an independent force in American banking. [92,93] The firm's first major triumph came during the financial panic of 1873, when Morgan demonstrated his ability to stabilize markets through decisive action. As smaller banks failed and stock prices plummeted, Morgan orchestrated a series of bold interventions, buying up depreciated railroad bonds and reorganizing failing companies. His actions earned him both profits and prestige, though critics would later point to this period as the beginning of his outsized influence over American finance.

Morgan's innovations in banking went far beyond traditional lending. He pioneered new methods of corporate reorganization, developing what became known as "Morganization" – the process of restructuring troubled companies through careful analysis, refinancing, and management changes. [91,92] This approach transformed American business practices and laid the groundwork for modern corporate restructuring.

The scale of Morgan's operations was unprecedented. By the 1880s, his firm was not just lending money but actively shaping industries. He created the first major electrical utility, Edison General Electric (later General Electric), and financed the modernization of the nation's railroads. [93,94] These projects required massive amounts of capital, which Morgan raised through innovative security offerings that helped create the modern bond market.

Yet Morgan's rise to power was not without controversy. His methods often involved creating what critics called "money trusts" – powerful combinations of banking interests that could control entire industries. [93,94] While Morgan argued that such consolidation brought stability and efficiency, others saw it as a dangerous concentration of economic power in private hands.

The tension between Morgan's private authority and public responsibility came to a head during the Panic of 1893. As the nation plunged into depression, Morgan orchestrated a private bailout of the U.S. Treasury, personally arranging a syndicate to supply the government with gold reserves. [93,33] This extraordinary intervention highlighted both the power of private bankers and the precarious nature of America's financial system.

Morgan's early career and innovations fundamentally altered American banking and continue to influence our financial system today. His emphasis on character in lending, though sometimes romanticized, established important principles of credit analysis. His methods of corporate reorganization became templates for modern bankruptcy procedures. Most significantly, the concentration of financial power that he represented ultimately led to the creation of the Federal Reserve System, as the nation recognized the need for public institutions to perform the stabilizing functions that Morgan had privately provided. [93,33]

The legacy of Morgan's early years extends beyond banking. His success represented a crucial shift in American power from commercial merchants to financial capitalists. The institutions he built –

particularly J.P. Morgan & Co. – became cornerstones of American finance, evolving into today's JPMorgan Chase. [92,93] His innovations in corporate finance, from bond offerings to merger techniques, remain fundamental to modern business practices.

Perhaps most importantly, Morgan's career embodied the transformative power of finance in industrializing America. Through his ability to mobilize vast sums of capital, he helped turn the United States from an agricultural nation into the world's leading industrial power. [91,92] The tension between private financial power and public interest that characterized his career continues to resonate in contemporary debates about banking regulation and economic policy, making his story as relevant today as it was in the Gilded Age.

Railroad Reorganization and Corporate Consolidation

"The first thing is character," J.P. Morgan once declared to a congressional committee. "Before money or anything else. Money cannot buy it." These words rang with particular irony across the grand marble halls of Wall Street in the 1880s, as Morgan orchestrated one of the most sweeping reorganizations of American industry in history – the great railroad consolidations that would reshape the nation's economic landscape.

In the winter of 1885, aboard his luxurious yacht Corsair, Morgan brokered a historic peace between the warring titans of the Pennsylvania Railroad and the New York Central Railroad. [95] The meeting, which took place over fine cigars and aged brandy, stood in stark contrast to the grim reality faced by railroad workers who endured twelve-hour shifts for mere dollars a day. [97] Yet this agreement would prove pivotal, ending a ruinous rate war that had threatened to destabilize the entire American railway system.

Morgan's intervention was not merely altruistic. By 1900, he would control approximately one-sixth of America's railroad network, [98] an empire of steel rails that stretched across the continent. His method of corporate reorganization transformed chaotic competition into ordered monopoly. When he encountered resistance, his power was absolute. 'I owe the public nothing,' he famously declared to one reporter who questioned his methods.

The scale of Morgan's railroad consolidations was unprecedented. Through his firm, J.P. Morgan & Co., he orchestrated the merger of numerous smaller railroads into powerful trunk lines. The creation of the Northern Securities Company in 1901 represented the pinnacle of this effort, combining major railroads into a near-monopoly that controlled transportation across the northwestern United States. [96] This consolidation was so complete that it eventually prompted President Theodore Roosevelt's 'trust-busting' campaign, leading to the landmark Northern Securities case that would help define the limits of corporate consolidation in America. [92]

The human cost of these consolidations was immense. As Morgan reorganized railroads, workers faced wage cuts and layoffs. The efficiency that shareholders celebrated often meant devastation for railroad towns that suddenly found themselves bypassed by new trunk lines. In 1886, when railroad workers across the Southwest went on strike against one of Morgan's reorganized lines, the response was swift and brutal. [97] The strike was crushed with the help of Pinkerton detectives and state militias, a pattern that would repeat itself across the industry.

Yet Morgan's railroad consolidations also brought undeniable benefits. The chaotic expansion of America's rail network, which had led to wasteful parallel lines and ruinous competition, [98] gave way to more efficient systems. Standard gauge tracks replaced the confusing variety of rail widths that had hindered interstate commerce. Improved safety standards and scheduling made rail travel more reliable for both passengers and freight. [96]

The impact of Morgan's railroad reorganizations extended far beyond the transportation sector. His methods of corporate consolidation became a template for industrial organization across America. The creation of U.S. Steel in 1901, capitalized at an unprecedented $1.4 billion, followed the same pattern of consolidation he had perfected in railroads. [99] This new model of corporate organization, with its professional management and widely traded shares, [99] would define American capitalism for the next century.

Morgan's consolidation of the railroads marked a crucial transition in American economic history. It represented the shift from an era of unfettered competition to one of managed competition under the oversight of powerful financial institutions. The public reaction to these consolidations – a mixture of awe at their efficiency and fear of their power – helped shape the American debate over corporate regulation that continues to this day.

Today, as we witness modern corporate mergers and debates over antitrust regulation, the echoes of Morgan's railroad consolidations remain clear. The tension between efficiency and competition, between private power and public interest, continues to define American capitalism. The rails that Morgan consolidated still crisscross the nation, now operated by corporations that trace their lineage to his reorganizations. [98] His legacy lives on in every merger review, every antitrust decision, and every debate over corporate power in American life.

The Creation of U.S. Steel: The First Billion-Dollar Corporation

"Put all your eggs in one basket and then watch that basket," Andrew Carnegie famously advised. On a cold February morning in 1901, J.P. Morgan stood in his opulent Madison Avenue office, preparing to create the world's first billion-dollar corporation. The deal he was orchestrating would transform not just American industry, but the very nature of corporate power. As Morgan lit his signature Havana cigar, the magnitude of the moment was not lost on him – he was about to purchase Andrew Carnegie's vast steel empire for $480 million, an unprecedented sum that would make the Scottish immigrant the richest man in the world. [100,101]

The creation of U.S. Steel marked the pinnacle of industrial consolidation in the Gilded Age. Morgan's vision went far beyond mere profit; he sought to bring order to the chaotic steel industry through massive consolidation. The numbers were staggering: $1.4 billion in capitalization, 168,000 workers, and control of 60-70% of America's steel market. To put this in perspective, the entire manufacturing sector of the United States was valued at just $9 billion at the time. [91,101]

The human drama behind this corporate behemoth was equally compelling. Carnegie, despite his immense wealth, signed away his steel empire on a simple sheet of paper, later telling Morgan, "Congratulations, Mr. Morgan, you are now the master of steel." [100] The deal was sealed over a handshake at Morgan's home, reflecting the personal nature of business at the highest levels of the Gilded Age. For Carnegie, it marked a transition from industrialist to philanthropist, as he would spend the rest of his life giving away his fortune.

Yet beneath the gleaming surface of this financial triumph lay a darker reality. The creation of U.S. Steel embodied the stark contrasts of the Gilded Age. While Morgan and Carnegie negotiated their billions, steel workers labored in dangerous conditions for mere dollars a day. The corporation's first president, Charles M. Schwab, earned an annual salary of $100,000 – an astronomical sum when compared to the average worker's wage of $500 per year. [100,102]

The formation of U.S. Steel represented more than just a business merger; it symbolized the triumph of financial capitalism over industrial capitalism. Morgan's ability to orchestrate such a massive consolidation demonstrated the growing power of Wall Street over America's industrial heart. [100,101] The corporation's creation sparked intense public debate about the concentration of economic power, leading to increased calls for government regulation.

The impact of U.S. Steel's formation rippled through American society. The corporation's vertical integration – controlling everything from iron ore mines to finished steel products – became a model for industrial organization. Its scale and efficiency helped position America as the world's leading industrial power, providing the steel that would build the nation's skyscrapers, bridges, and railroads. [102]

In the elegant boardrooms of Wall Street, the deal was celebrated as a masterpiece of financial engineering. Yet in the steel towns of Pennsylvania and Ohio, workers viewed the consolidation with apprehension. Their fears were not unfounded – U.S. Steel would become known for its fierce resistance to unionization and its use of private security forces to suppress labor unrest. [91,33]

The creation of U.S. Steel marked a watershed moment in American capitalism. It demonstrated both the productive potential and the social costs of industrial consolidation. [100,91] The corporation's formation helped establish patterns of corporate organization, labor relations, and government regulation that would shape American business for decades to come. Today, as we grapple with questions of corporate power, income inequality, and the role of government in regulating business, the story of U.S. Steel's creation remains remarkably relevant.

The legacy of this first billion-dollar corporation extends far beyond its immediate impact on the steel industry. It set precedents for corporate mergers, established new relationships between finance and industry, and raised fundamental questions about economic power in a democratic society – questions that continue to resonate in our own time. [100,101] As modern corporations grow to unprecedented size and influence, the lessons of U.S. Steel's creation – both its achievements and its controversies – offer valuable insights into the ongoing debate about the proper balance between corporate power and public interest.

The Panic of 1907: Private Power and Public Interest

"A man always has two reasons for doing anything: a good reason and the real reason." - J.P. Morgan

On October 22, 1907, the marble halls of the Knickerbocker Trust Company echoed with the desperate footsteps of depositors rushing to withdraw their savings. The scene was chaos incarnate – wealthy socialites stood shoulder-to-shoulder with factory workers, all united in their panic. By day's end, the Knickerbocker, one of New York's largest trust companies, had paid out more than $8 million to frightened depositors before closing its doors forever. [103,106] This was not just another bank run; it was the beginning of a financial tsunami that would threaten to destroy America's entire economic system.

Meanwhile, in his opulent library on Madison Avenue, J.P. Morgan received an urgent message from the Knickerbocker's president, Charles Barney. The trust company was on the brink of collapse, and only Morgan's intervention could save it. Yet Morgan, after examining the Knickerbocker's books, made the cold calculation to let it fail. [103,104] This decision, while brutal, exemplified Morgan's approach to the crisis – he would save the financial system, but not every institution within it.

As panic spread through New York's financial district, the contrast between Wall Street's marble palaces and the growing bread lines in the city's working-class neighborhoods became stark. The crisis laid bare the fragility of America's unregulated banking system, where the fate of millions rested in the hands of a few private bankers. [104,105] Morgan transformed his library into a command center, summoning the nation's leading financiers to coordinate a response to the growing crisis.

In one of the most dramatic episodes of the panic, Morgan locked forty-odd bankers in his library late one night, refusing to let them leave until they had pledged $25 million to save the Trust Company of America, the next institution in the panic's crosshairs. [103,104] "Tomorrow will be too late," Morgan thundered at the assembled financiers, compelling them to sign agreements before they could depart. This extraordinary display of private power proved effective – by morning, the rescue package was in place.

The crisis reached its apex when the New York Stock Exchange nearly collapsed. Morgan again intervened, this time providing $25 million in loans to keep the exchange open. [103,104,33] He even authorized his associates to use his personal funds to purchase stock, helping to halt the market's slide. When President Theodore Roosevelt's administration tacitly approved Morgan's emergency takeover of Tennessee Coal, Iron and Railroad Company by U.S. Steel – despite antitrust concerns – it marked an unprecedented cooperation between private financial power and public authority. [103,104,33]

Yet Morgan's heroic intervention came at a price. The sight of one private citizen wielding such enormous power over the nation's economy deeply disturbed many Americans. [104,105] As one contemporary journalist noted, "The fact that one man had it in his power to save or to wreck the nation's business fabric was intolerable." This sentiment would help drive the creation of the Federal Reserve System in 1913, finally establishing a public institution to manage such crises. [104,105,106]

The human cost of the panic was immense. In the months following the crisis, unemployment soared to 8%, with industrial production falling by 11%. [103,104] The working class, already struggling with low wages and poor conditions, bore the brunt of the economic contraction. While Morgan coordinated bailouts from his marble-clad library, workers faced layoffs, wage cuts, and the constant fear of destitution.

The Panic of 1907 marked a crucial turning point in American financial history. It demonstrated both the extraordinary power of private banking and its fundamental inadequacy in managing a modern industrial economy. [104,33,106] The crisis led directly to the creation of the Federal Reserve System, establishing the framework of banking regulation that continues to shape our financial system today. The tension between private financial power and public interest that Morgan embodied remains a central challenge in modern America, as debates over banking regulation, economic inequality, and the role of government in managing financial crises continue to echo the lessons of 1907.

As we witness modern financial crises and debates over banking regulation, the ghost of 1907 looms large. The questions it raised –

about the concentration of financial power, the role of government in managing economic stability, and the balance between private initiative and public interest – remain as relevant today as they were in Morgan's time. The marble halls of Wall Street still stand, but now they operate under the watchful eye of public institutions born from the crucible of that fateful autumn.

Art Collection and Cultural Influence: Morgan as a Cultural Force

"A man's purchases of pictures or books or statuary for his own enjoyment should not be considered philanthropy, but rather a phase of his own education and culture." - J.P. Morgan

On a crisp autumn evening in 1906, J.P. Morgan stood in his newly completed library on Madison Avenue, surrounded by illuminated manuscripts, rare books, and priceless artworks. The marble floors gleamed beneath the soft glow of electric lights – a modern touch in this Renaissance-inspired sanctuary. This was no mere collection of beautiful objects; it was Morgan's vision of American cultural ascendancy made manifest in stone, steel, and parchment.

Morgan's passion for collecting went far beyond the typical acquisitiveness of the wealthy. Over just twenty-three years, he amassed more than 20,000 objects, spending what would amount to approximately $900 million in today's currency. [107] His collection ranged from ancient Assyrian tablets to medieval religious relics, including a tooth purportedly belonging to Mary Magdalene. The scale and scope of his acquisitions were staggering – Raphael's Colonna Altarpiece, precious illuminated manuscripts, Gutenberg Bibles, and handwritten scores by Mozart and Beethoven all found their way into his possession. [108]

The construction of his library, designed by the prestigious firm of McKim, Mead & White, represented the pinnacle of this cultural ambition. Its palazzo-style architecture and hidden steel vault embodied both Morgan's wealth and his dedication to preservation. [107] Yet this was no mere temple to private indulgence. Morgan understood that great art and culture should serve a broader purpose. As he once remarked to a friend while surveying his collection, "The ownership of a fine thing carries with it the obligation to share it."

As President of the Metropolitan Museum of Art, Morgan worked tirelessly to transform the institution into a world-class museum. His influence extended beyond mere financial support – he actively shaped the Met's collection policy and institutional direction. By his death in 1913, he had helped establish the museum as one of the world's premier cultural institutions. The subsequent donation of approximately 7,000 pieces from his collection to the Met would forever change the landscape of American art. [108]

Yet Morgan's cultural influence was not without its critics. His collecting habits heavily favored European masters and religious art, often overlooking American artists and modern works. This Eurocentric focus reflected both his personal tastes and a broader cultural anxiety among America's elite – a desire to connect their new nation to the grand traditions of European civilization. [108] While Morgan was building his collection, many American artists struggled to find patrons and recognition in their own country.

The transformation of Morgan's private library into a public institution after his death marked a crucial shift in American cultural life. His son Jack's decision to open the collection to the public created what would become the Morgan Library & Museum, establishing a model for private collections becoming public resources. [108] The hidden staircases and secret vaults that once protected Morgan's treasures now served as pathways for public access to cultural knowledge. [107]

Morgan's influence on American culture extended beyond his collecting. His example inspired other wealthy individuals to support the arts and established patterns of cultural philanthropy that continue to shape American institutions today. The tension between private wealth and public access, between European tradition and American innovation, that characterized Morgan's cultural activities remains relevant to contemporary debates about art, wealth, and social responsibility.

Today, as we witness debates over the role of private wealth in supporting public culture, Morgan's legacy offers important insights. The institutions he helped build – from the Metropolitan Museum to the Morgan Library – continue to serve as vital cultural resources. Yet they also remind us of the complex relationship between private power and public good that defined the Gilded Age and continues to shape American society. Morgan's cultural legacy, like his financial one, remains both inspiring and problematic, a testament to the enduring questions about wealth, culture, and social responsibility in American life.

Legacy: The Birth of the Federal Reserve System

"The ownership of wealth carries with it an obligation to use it in a responsible way." - J.P. Morgan, testifying before Congress, 1912

The marble halls of J.P. Morgan's library stood silent on that fateful December morning in 1913, as President Woodrow Wilson signed into law the Federal Reserve Act. [109,110,111] The legislation marked the end of an era – one where private bankers like Morgan had served as the nation's de facto central bank. The irony was not lost on those present: The very power that Morgan had wielded during the Panic of 1907 had ultimately led to its own displacement by a federal institution. [109,111]

The creation of the Federal Reserve System emerged directly from the ashes of the 1907 financial crisis, where Morgan's personal intervention had saved the American economy from collapse. [109,111] In the aftermath of that panic, even Morgan himself recognized the precariousness of a financial system that depended on the resources and judgment of a single private citizen. "I am afraid," he had confided to a close associate, "that someday the people will understand the power of the banking system."

The National Monetary Commission, established in 1908, embarked on an unprecedented study of global banking systems. [109,111] Its members traveled across Europe, examining the central banks of Britain, France, and Germany. The contrast they found was stark – while European nations had developed sophisticated central banking systems, America's financial structure remained a patchwork of competing interests and unstable currencies. [109] The Commission's findings painted a clear picture: The United States needed a modern central banking system to prevent future crises.

Yet the path to creating the Federal Reserve was anything but smooth. In the marbled corridors of Congress and the wood-paneled boardrooms of Wall Street, fierce debates raged over the proper balance between public oversight and private control. [109,110] The ghost of Andrew Jackson's war against the Second Bank of the United States still haunted these discussions, as did fresh memories of the "money trust" investigations that had exposed the concentrated power of Wall Street banks.

The final structure of the Federal Reserve System represented a uniquely American compromise – twelve regional Reserve Banks, owned by member banks but overseen by a government-appointed Board of Governors. [109,110,111] This decentralized structure addressed both the fear of concentrated financial power and the need for coordinated national monetary policy. The system would provide an "elastic currency" that could expand or contract based on economic conditions, addressing one of the key weaknesses that had plagued the American economy. [110,111]

The impact of the Federal Reserve's creation extended far beyond banking. It marked a fundamental shift in the relationship between private wealth and public power in America. [10,111] No longer would the nation's financial stability depend on the personal resources and decisions of private bankers like Morgan. Instead, a public institution would assume responsibility for managing the money supply and providing stability during economic crises. [10,111]

The establishment of the Federal Reserve also reflected broader changes in American society. The Progressive Era's emphasis on professional expertise and scientific management found expression in the Fed's structure, which combined technical expertise with public accountability. [109] The system's creation acknowledged that in a modern industrial economy, financial stability was too important to be left to private interests alone.

Today, as debates continue over the Federal Reserve's role and independence, the echoes of its creation resonate strongly. [109,110] The tension between private financial power and public oversight remains at the heart of American economic policy. The Fed's dual mandate – to maintain price stability while promoting maximum employment – continues to reflect the Progressive Era's belief that government institutions could balance competing social interests. [111]

The Federal Reserve's birth marked the end of the Gilded Age's purely private financial power and the beginning of modern American banking. [109,111] Its creation established patterns of institutional oversight that would later expand during the New Deal and beyond. As we grapple with contemporary financial challenges, from digital currencies to global economic integration, the lessons of the Fed's founding remind us that financial innovation must be balanced with public accountability and systematic oversight.

Morgan's library, now a museum, stands as a testament to this transformation. Its magnificent rooms, once the command center of private financial power, now welcome public visitors. The very space where Morgan once decided the fate of banks and corporations during the Panic of 1907 [109,111] serves as a reminder of how far America's financial system has evolved. The Federal Reserve's creation marked not just the end of an era, but the beginning of modern American finance – a legacy that continues to shape our economic life today. J.P. Morgan's impact on American finance and society extends far beyond the marble halls of his Madison Avenue library or the boardrooms of Wall Street. His story embodied both the extraordinary potential and the inherent dangers of concentrated private power in an industrializing nation. As we've seen throughout this chapter, Morgan's influence reached into every corner of American life – from the railroads that crossed the continent to the artwork that graced museum walls, from the steel mills that built modern cities to the banking system that would ultimately give birth to the Federal Reserve.

The Panic of 1907 serves as perhaps the most telling illustration of Morgan's complex legacy. His ability to single-handedly save the American economy demonstrated both the remarkable capabilities of private initiative and the precarious nature of a financial system dependent on individual actors. The sight of the nation's most powerful financiers locked in Morgan's library until they agreed to support failing banks captured the public's imagination and spurred crucial reforms. The creation of the Federal Reserve System in 1913 marked a fundamental shift in American banking – a recognition that in a modern industrial economy, financial stability required institutional oversight rather than the judgment of a single "Jupiter."

Morgan's consolidation of American industry through ventures like U.S. Steel and his railroad reorganizations reshaped the nation's economic landscape. These efforts brought efficiency and stability but also raised troubling questions about the concentration of economic power – questions that continue to resonate in contemporary debates about corporate influence and regulation. His cultural patronage, embodied in institutions like the Metropolitan Museum of Art and his own library, established patterns of private support for public culture that remain influential today.

As we reflect on Morgan's era from our contemporary vantage point, the parallels are striking. Today's debates about financial regulation, corporate power, and the role of private wealth in public life echo the controversies of the Gilded Age. The tension between private initiative and public oversight, between individual power and institutional control, remains at the heart of American economic life. Morgan's legacy serves as both inspiration and warning – a reminder of the productive potential of private enterprise and the essential role of public oversight in modern capitalism.

Perhaps most importantly, Morgan's story illuminates the complex relationship between private power and public interest in American society. His career demonstrated how individual charisma could mobilize resources and transform industries, but also how such concentrated power could threaten democratic values. The institutions that emerged in response to his era – from the Federal Reserve to antitrust laws – continue to shape our economic life, while the questions his career raised about wealth, power, and social responsibility remain remarkably relevant.

In many ways, modern America still lives in the shadow of Morgan's library. The financial systems he helped create, the cultural institutions he supported, and the corporate structures he pioneered continue to influence our world. Yet his era also reminds us that change is possible – that societies can reform themselves in response to the challenges of concentrated power. As we face our own questions about economic inequality, corporate influence, and financial stability, Morgan's story offers both cautionary lessons and hope for constructive change.

The echoes of the Gilded Age resonate clearly in our modern world of global finance, corporate mergers, and debates over economic inequality. Just as Morgan's generation grappled with the challenges of industrial capitalism, we face the complexities of a digital economy and global markets. The solutions they found – balanced between private initiative and public oversight – may offer guidance as we address our own economic challenges. In this way, Morgan's legacy continues to shape our understanding of wealth, power, and responsibility in American society.

CHAPTER FIVE

The Astor Legacy: From Fur Trade to Fifth Avenue's Golden Mile

In 1784, a young German immigrant named John Jacob Astor stepped onto New York's shores with seven flutes and a dream, unaware that he would establish America's first great fortune and transform a growing city into a world capital. Through shrewd investments in fur trading and Manhattan real estate, Astor would amass a fortune worth over $20 million by 1848 (equivalent to billions today), laying the foundation for a dynasty that would define New York's social and architectural landscape for generations. "In matters of fashion and society, one must either lead or follow," Caroline Astor once declared, a sentiment that perfectly captured the Astor family's commanding role in New York society. Through generations of careful investment and social maneuvering, the Astors had transformed themselves from merchant traders into America's premier family, their name synonymous with wealth, power, and social prestige.

The family's rise paralleled New York's own transformation from a bustling port town into a global metropolis. As Manhattan expanded northward, the Astors' prescient real estate investments turned acres of farmland into prime urban property, creating an empire of hotels, apartments, and commercial buildings that would generate wealth for generations. Their real estate strategy was deceptively simple yet remarkably effective: buy land far ahead of development, wait for the city to grow, and profit immensely from urbanization.

But it was in the realm of society that the Astors, particularly Caroline Astor, wielded their most profound influence. As New York's population swelled with newly-minted millionaires from industry and finance, Caroline Astor emerged as the ultimate arbiter of social status, determining who would be accepted into the highest circles of society. Her famous list of "The 400" – supposedly the number of people that could fit in her ballroom – became the definitive roster of New York's elite.

In January 1883, this social power reached its zenith at Caroline Astor's annual ball, an event that would forever crystallize the family's role in American society. The carefully curated guest list of exactly 400 people represented what Mrs. Astor and her social secretary Ward McAllister deemed the cream of New York society. That evening, as the city's elite gathered in her opulent Fifth Avenue mansion, the very concept of American aristocracy was being codified.

The ball showcased the culmination of the Astor family's remarkable transformation. From John Jacob's humble beginnings as a fur trader to Caroline's reign as the undisputed queen of society, the Astors had achieved something unprecedented in American history: the creation of an unofficial aristocracy in a supposedly democratic nation. When Ward McAllister famously declared that there were "only about 400 people in fashionable New York Society," he was doing more than making a casual observation – he was establishing a social hierarchy that would influence American society for decades to come.

Newspapers across the country breathlessly reported every detail of the ball, from the elaborate decorations to the strict social protocols observed. The evening's events demonstrated not only the Astors' social supremacy but also cemented New York's position as America's cultural capital. The meticulous attention paid to who was included – and perhaps more importantly, who was excluded – revealed how thoroughly the Astors had shaped New York's social landscape.

This transformation from merchants to social arbiters reflected a broader shift in American society, as old money families like the Astors grappled with the emergence of new industrial fortunes. Their story illuminates the complex dynamics of class, wealth, and social status that defined the Gilded Age and continues to resonate in American society today. Through their real estate empire and social influence, the Astors helped create a distinctly American form of aristocracy, one based not on hereditary titles but on the power of wealth and social connections.

John Jacob Astor's Rise: From Fur Trading to Real Estate Empire

"In America, a man's wealth is measured not by what he has, but by what he can acquire." These words, spoken by John Jacob Astor to a business associate in 1817, captured the essence of his meteoric rise from humble immigrant to America's first multi-millionaire. On a bitter winter morning in 1784, when Astor first set foot on American soil with just seven flutes and $25 in his pocket, [115,118,119] few could have predicted that this young German immigrant would fundamentally reshape New York's economic landscape.

Astor's early days in New York were marked by careful observation and calculated risk-taking. Working first as a butcher's assistant and then as a flute seller, he spent hours at the bustling New York harbor, watching merchants trade and learning the intricacies of commerce. It was here that he first noticed the lucrative potential of the fur trade, observing how pelts purchased for mere dollars in the American frontier could command princely sums in European markets.

By 1786, he had established his first fur trading venture, making arduous journeys into the wilderness to negotiate directly with Native American trappers. [116,118] His ability to forge relationships with Indigenous peoples, combined with his shrewd business acumen, set him apart from competitors. One particularly pivotal moment came in 1794 when the Jay Treaty opened trade routes between the United States and British-controlled Canada. Astor, recognizing the opportunity before many others, quickly established a network of trading posts throughout the Great Lakes region. [115,118,120]

The founding of the American Fur Company in 1808 marked Astor's emergence as a dominant force in American commerce. Through this enterprise, he effectively created America's first business monopoly, controlling fur trading routes from the Great Lakes to the Pacific Northwest. [115,119,120] His ruthless efficiency in eliminating competitors earned him both admiration and enmity – when smaller traders complained about his tactics, Astor famously remarked, "Competition is a sin."

However, it was Astor's transition from fur trading to Manhattan real estate that truly cemented his legacy. As New York City began its northward expansion in the early 1800s, Astor made a series of prescient land purchases that would multiply in value as the city grew. [116,118,119] He bought vast tracts of Manhattan farmland well ahead of development, often facing ridicule for acquiring what seemed like worthless property. Yet as the city expanded, these investments proved extraordinarily profitable.

One of Astor's most successful strategies involved leasing rather than selling his properties. He would lease land to developers who would construct buildings at their own expense. After the lease expired, typically 21 years, Astor would reclaim both the land and any improvements made to it. This approach ensured a steady income stream while maintaining long-term control over his real estate empire.

By the 1830s, Astor had largely withdrawn from the fur trade, focusing instead on his real estate holdings. [116,118,119] His timing proved impeccable – as New York's population exploded from 60,000 in 1800 to over 300,000 by 1840, his property values soared. At the time of his death in 1848, Astor's fortune of $20 million (equivalent to billions today) made him America's wealthiest individual, with much of that wealth derived from Manhattan real estate. [115,119]

Astor's influence extended beyond mere commerce. His success story helped establish New York as America's financial capital and created a template for future business titans. His strategic approach to real estate investment – buying ahead of development and maintaining long-term control through leasing – continues to influence property development strategies today. The Astor fortune would go on to shape New York's cultural landscape through the creation of institutions like the Astor Library, which later became part of the New York Public Library system. [119]

Perhaps most significantly, Astor's rise embodied the American Dream while simultaneously revealing its contradictions. His success demonstrated the possibilities for social mobility in the young republic, yet his monopolistic practices and accumulation of vast wealth also highlighted the potential for economic inequality in an unregulated capitalist system. [117,119,121] These tensions would later fuel Progressive Era reforms and continue to resonate in debates about wealth concentration and economic opportunity in modern America.

The legacy of John Jacob Astor's remarkable transformation from immigrant merchant to real estate mogul lives on in contemporary New York. His strategic vision for Manhattan's development helped establish patterns of urban growth that shaped the modern city. The Astor name became synonymous with New York real estate, setting a precedent for how wealth could be created and maintained through property ownership – a model that continues to influence real estate investment strategies today. His story remains a compelling testament to both the opportunities and contradictions of American capitalism, offering insights that remain relevant in our ongoing debates about wealth, opportunity, and the American Dream.

The Astor Real Estate Strategy: Buying Manhattan's Future

"Buy land," John Jacob Astor once advised a young protégé, "they're not making it anymore." This simple yet profound observation underpinned what would become one of the most successful real estate strategies in American history. On a crisp autumn morning in 1810, as Astor stood atop a hill in what would later become midtown Manhattan, he gazed across miles of undeveloped farmland stretching northward. Where others saw only scattered settlements and grazing cattle, Astor envisioned a metropolis of commerce and culture that would rival the great cities of Europe.

Astor's revolutionary approach to real estate investment would transform not only his family's fortunes but the very fabric of Manhattan itself. Rather than following the conventional wisdom of investing in already-developed areas, Astor focused on acquiring vast tracts of undeveloped land well ahead of the city's northward expansion. [122,127] His most significant coup came with the acquisition of the 22-acre Eden Farm near present-day Times Square – obtained through a shrewd foreclosure deal. This single property, later subdivided into 141 lots, would eventually sell for an astounding $5.1 million, generating one of the most profitable real estate transactions of the era. [126]

But perhaps Astor's most innovative contribution to real estate strategy was his pioneering use of the leasehold system. Instead of selling properties outright, he preferred to lease them long-term, maintaining ownership of the increasingly valuable land while generating steady rental income. [126,127] This approach, which became known as the "Astor method," would influence New York real estate practices for generations to come. When questioned about this strategy by a business associate, Astor reportedly replied, "The rents of New York will one day make me richer than any sovereign in Europe."

The timing of Astor's investments proved remarkably prescient. As New York City's population exploded from 60,000 in 1800 to over 300,000 by 1840, his carefully chosen properties appreciated dramatically in value. His strategy of buying during economic downturns, when others were selling in panic, allowed him to amass an unprecedented portfolio of prime Manhattan real estate. [126] During the Panic of 1837, while other investors retreated, Astor doubled down on his investments, acquiring distressed properties at bargain prices.

However, Astor's real estate empire was not without its controversies. His role as a landlord often drew criticism, particularly regarding the conditions in his lower-income properties. [123,126] The contrast between the opulent Astor House hotel – New York's first luxury hotel – and the crowded tenements he owned in lower Manhattan highlighted the stark inequalities of the era. Yet even his critics couldn't deny the transformative impact of his vision on Manhattan's development.

Astor's influence extended beyond mere property ownership. His strategic donations of land for public institutions, such as the Astor Library, helped shape the cultural landscape of the city. [127] The development of Astor Place became a symbol of the city's northward expansion and cultural aspirations, while his commercial properties helped establish Manhattan as America's premier business center.

The legacy of Astor's real estate strategy continues to influence modern Manhattan. His "never sell" philosophy and emphasis on long-term property ownership remain foundational principles in New York real estate. [126] The Astor family's approach to urban development – combining commercial success with cultural institution-building – created a template for how private wealth could shape public spaces and civic life.

Perhaps most significantly, Astor's strategy demonstrated the potential for real estate to generate dynastic wealth in America. His success inspired subsequent generations of developers and investors, from the Vanderbilts to modern-day real estate moguls. [125,126] The patterns of urban development he established – particularly the relationship between transportation infrastructure and property values – continue to influence city planning and real estate investment strategies today.

In modern Manhattan, where real estate remains one of the most powerful engines of wealth creation, the echoes of Astor's vision are everywhere. [124,127] From the enduring practice of long-term ground leases to the strategic timing of property acquisitions, his innovations have become standard practices in real estate investment. The Astor legacy reminds us that the physical shape of our cities – and the distribution of wealth within them – often reflects the strategic decisions of far-sighted investors who saw value where others saw only vacant land.

Caroline Astor and the Creation of 'The 400'

"Society is like a lawn, where every roughness is smoothed, every bramble eradicated, and where the eye is delighted by the smiling verdure of a velvet surface," Caroline Astor once declared, perfectly capturing her vision for New York's social hierarchy. On a bitter January evening in 1883, as the city's elite gathered for her annual winter ball, Mrs. Astor stood at the entrance of her opulent Fifth Avenue mansion, presiding over what would become the most exclusive social event in American history. [130,131] That night, through the careful curation of her guest list, she would formally establish "The Four Hundred" – the definitive roster of New York's social elite.

Caroline Schermerhorn Astor's rise to social prominence was as calculated as it was complete. Born into an old Dutch family in 1830, [128,129] her marriage to William Backhouse Astor Jr. combined old-world lineage with new-world wealth. As New York's population swelled with newly-minted millionaires from industry and finance, Caroline recognized the need to establish clear social boundaries. With the help of her trusted advisor Ward McAllister, she set about creating a codified system of social hierarchy that would define Gilded Age New York. [128,132]

The concept of "The Four Hundred" emerged from McAllister's famous assertion that there were "only about 400 people in fashionable New York Society." While popular legend tied this number to the capacity of Mrs. Astor's ballroom, the figure actually represented McAllister's careful calculation of those families with sufficient pedigree and refinement to be considered truly "fashionable." [129,132] The list became a powerful tool for social control, allowing Caroline to maintain the exclusivity of old-money circles while selectively incorporating acceptable nouveau riche families. [128,129]

Caroline's annual balls were masterpieces of social engineering. Each detail was carefully orchestrated to reinforce the hierarchies she had established. The evening would begin with a nine-course dinner featuring elaborate French cuisine, followed by dancing that continued until dawn. The guest list was scrutinized with diplomatic precision – an invitation could make or break a family's social standing. [130,131] Even the Vanderbilts, despite their enormous wealth, were initially excluded until Alva Vanderbilt's strategic maneuvering forced Caroline to acknowledge them. [128,131]

The ritual of "calling cards" became another instrument of social control. Ladies would make formal visits, leaving their cards with the butler. Caroline would then sort through these cards, deciding which visits to return – a process that effectively determined who would be admitted to society. [128,129] This system created a complex web of social obligations and hierarchies that dominated New York life. As one contemporary observer noted, "Mrs. Astor's calling card was worth more than a letter of introduction from the President."

However, Caroline's reign as the arbiter of society was not without its challenges. The publication of the Four Hundred list in The New York Times in 1892 – a tactical error by McAllister – exposed the previously private machinations of social gatekeeping to public scrutiny. [131,132] The list revealed the complex balance between old and new money, including both ancient Knickerbocker families and more recent industrial fortunes deemed sufficiently refined for inclusion. [129,132]

The contrast between these elaborate social rituals and the reality of Gilded Age New York was stark. While Caroline's balls consumed vast sums on flowers, food, and entertainment, [130,131] just blocks away, immigrants crowded into tenements, and workers struggled in dangerous factories. This juxtaposition highlighted the growing inequalities of the era and would eventually contribute to calls for social reform.

Caroline Astor's creation of The Four Hundred represented more than mere social exclusivity – it was an attempt to create an American aristocracy in a democratic nation. [128,129] Through her careful curation of society, she established patterns of social stratification that would influence American culture well beyond the Gilded Age. The concept of social registers, exclusive clubs, and carefully regulated admission to high society would persist throughout the twentieth century.

The legacy of Caroline Astor and The Four Hundred continues to resonate in contemporary American society. The tension between old and new money, the role of social gatekeepers, and the power of exclusive networks remain relevant in today's discussions of wealth and social mobility. [128,129] Modern social media influencers and celebrity culture echo the carefully curated world of Caroline Astor, while exclusive social clubs and organizations continue to function as modern-day equivalents of her famous list. Her story serves as a reminder that in America, even in a supposedly democratic society, social hierarchies can be as rigid and influential as any aristocratic system of the Old World.

Architectural Legacy: The Astor Hotels and Fifth Avenue Mansions

"Architecture is frozen music," declared William Waldorf Astor in 1893, standing before his newly completed Waldorf Hotel on Fifth Avenue. "And I intend to compose a symphony in stone." This architectural ambition would reshape Manhattan's skyline and redefine American luxury, setting standards that would influence hospitality and residential architecture for generations to come.

On a crisp autumn morning in 1836, New York's elite gathered for the grand opening of the Astor House, John Jacob Astor's revolutionary venture into luxury hospitality. The six-story granite building, occupying an entire city block on Broadway between Vesey and Barclay Streets, represented a radical departure from the modest inns and taverns that had previously served the city. With its imposing Greek Revival façade, featuring massive Doric columns and innovative amenities like private rooms with locks, gaslights, and bathing facilities on every floor, [136,139] the Astor House established new standards for American hotels.

The hotel's opening ceremony captured the stark contrasts of Gilded Age society. While distinguished guests marveled at the cast-iron and glass rotunda, [136,139] hundreds of curious onlookers gathered outside, pressing their faces against the windows to glimpse the unprecedented luxury within. One observer noted that the cost of a single night's stay at the Astor House exceeded a working family's monthly rent in the nearby Five Points district.

However, it was the creation of the Waldorf-Astoria Hotel in the 1890s that truly epitomized the Astor family's architectural ambitions and internal rivalries. The hotel's genesis stemmed from a famous family feud – William Waldorf Astor's decision to demolish his father's mansion at Fifth Avenue and 33rd Street to build the Waldorf Hotel was partly motivated by his desire to spite his aunt Caroline Astor, who lived next door. The thirteen-story Waldorf, designed by Henry Janeway Hardenbergh, opened in 1893, featuring unprecedented luxuries and technological innovations. [134,138]

Four years later, John Jacob Astor IV, not to be outdone by his cousin, erected the even grander Astoria Hotel on the adjacent plot where his mother's mansion had stood. The two hotels were connected by the famous 'Peacock Alley,' a 300-foot marble corridor that became the see-and-be-seen promenade of New York society. [134,137] The combined Waldorf-Astoria complex revolutionized American hospitality, introducing concepts we now take for granted – room service, private bathrooms, and the concept of the 'grand hotel' as a social institution. [123]

The Astor family's residential architecture was equally influential. Caroline Astor's mansion at 350 Fifth Avenue, with its relatively understated exterior but lavishly appointed interiors, established the template for Gilded Age urban palaces. The ballroom, designed to accommodate her famous 'Four Hundred,' became the model for subsequent Fifth Avenue mansions. [138] When John Jacob Astor IV later built his twin residences at Fifth Avenue and 65th Street, designed by Richard Morris Hunt, they represented the pinnacle of residential luxury, featuring twin grand staircases and interconnected ballrooms that could host the city's largest social gatherings. [135]

Yet these architectural monuments also reflected the era's deep social divisions. While the Waldorf-Astoria's kitchen staff worked fourteen-hour days in sweltering conditions, wealthy guests above dined on elaborate French cuisine served on gold-rimmed Limoges china. The hotel's construction itself displaced dozens of working-class families, a pattern repeated throughout the city as luxury development pushed northward.

The Hotel Astor, opened in 1904 in Times Square, represented the family's adaptation to changing times. This Beaux-Arts masterpiece by Clinton & Russell featured modern amenities while maintaining the grandeur expected of the Astor name. Its roof garden became a popular entertainment venue, [133,137] democratizing luxury in a way the earlier Astor properties had not.

The architectural legacy of the Astors' extends far beyond the physical structures they built. Though most of their original buildings have been demolished – the original Waldorf-Astoria making way for the Empire State Building, [134,137] the Hotel Astor replaced by One Astor Plaza [133] – their influence on American architecture and hospitality remains profound. They established enduring standards for luxury accommodations, helped define the concept of the urban hotel as a social center, and demonstrated how architecture could be used as an expression of wealth and power.

Today, as we witness the construction of new luxury towers along 'Billionaires' Row' near Central Park, we see echoes of the Astors' architectural ambitions. The modern super-tall residential buildings, like their Gilded Age predecessors, serve as both homes and symbols of wealth and status. The Astor legacy reminds us that in New York, architecture has always been inextricably linked with power, prestige, and the complex social hierarchies that continue to shape our urban landscape.

The Astor Family's Influence on New York Society and Culture

"Society is like a lawn, where every roughness is smoothed, every bramble eradicated, and where the eye is delighted by the smiling verdure of a velvet surface." These words, spoken by Caroline Astor in 1872, perfectly captured the calculated artifice of New York's social hierarchy that the Astor family helped create and maintain for nearly a century. Their influence extended far beyond mere wealth, reshaping the very fabric of American society and culture in ways that continue to resonate today.

On that bitter January evening in 1883, as Caroline Astor stood in her opulent Fifth Avenue mansion surveying the glittering assemblage of New York's elite at her annual winter ball, she presided over more than just a social gathering – she was orchestrating the very definition of American aristocracy. [141,142] The contrast between the lavish festivities inside and the harsh winter conditions endured by the working class just blocks away epitomized the stark social divisions of the Gilded Age. While guests dined on French delicacies served on gold-rimmed Limoges china, immigrant families in nearby tenements struggled to afford basic necessities.

The Astors' influence on New York society was both deliberate and profound. Through Caroline's famous 'Four Hundred' – her carefully curated list of acceptable society members – she established a social hierarchy that would influence American culture for generations. The number was supposedly chosen because 400 was the capacity of her ballroom, but in reality, it represented Ward McAllister's calculation of those families with sufficient pedigree and refinement to be considered truly 'fashionable.' [141,142,144] This system of social stratification created an unofficial American aristocracy, complete with its own customs, rituals, and codes of behavior.

The family's impact extended well beyond social circles. The Astor Library, founded by John Jacob Astor's son William Backhouse Astor Sr., formed the cornerstone of what would become the New York Public Library. [140,145,124] This institution democratized access to knowledge and literature, though ironically, it was funded by wealth accumulated through often ruthless business practices. The Astor Opera House became a symbol of cultural refinement, [142,123] even as it highlighted the growing divide between the city's elite and working classes.

The Astors' philanthropic efforts, while significant, often served dual purposes. Their support of cultural institutions like the Metropolitan Opera helped establish New York as a global cultural capital, [142,143] but it also reinforced their position at the apex of society. The family's donations to educational initiatives and public libraries reflected a complex mix of genuine civic mindedness and strategic social positioning. [123,145,124]

The influence of the Astor family extended into the very geography of New York City. Astor Place and Astoria, Queens still bear their name, [123,124] while countless buildings and institutions stand as testament to their legacy. Their real estate holdings shaped the physical development of Manhattan, as their strategic land purchases and development decisions influenced patterns of urban growth that continue to affect the city today. [123,124]

The decline of the Astor family's direct influence coincided with broader social changes in American society. The Great Depression, two World Wars, and changing attitudes toward inherited wealth and social privilege gradually eroded the rigid social hierarchies they had helped establish. Yet their legacy persists in unexpected ways – from the social registers that still track America's upper class to the complex relationship between wealth, culture, and social status that continues to shape American society. [143,123]

Today, as we witness the rise of new tech billionaires and debate questions of wealth inequality and social mobility, the story of the Astor family's influence on New York society and culture offers important insights. Their legacy reminds us that the intersection of wealth, culture, and social status remains as complex and contentious today as it was during the Gilded Age. The institutions they helped establish – from the New York Public Library to the Metropolitan Opera – continue to enrich the cultural life of the city, [142,145] even as we grapple with questions about the role of private wealth in public spaces and cultural institutions.

The Astor family's story ultimately reveals how thoroughly private wealth can shape public culture, for better and worse. Their influence on New York society created patterns of social stratification and cultural patronage that continue to influence American life, making their legacy a crucial lens through which to understand both the achievements and contradictions of American society.

Generational Wealth: The Evolution of the Astor Fortune

"Money is like manure; it's not worth a thing unless it's spread around encouraging young things to grow." These words, spoken by Brooke

Astor in 1980, reflected a profound shift in how America's first great fortune evolved across generations, from ruthless accumulation to philanthropic distribution. [149,145] The transformation of the Astor fortune from John Jacob's initial $25 investment to America's first multi-million dollar empire remains one of the most fascinating stories of wealth creation and evolution in American history.

On a frigid morning in 1783, when John Jacob Astor first stepped onto New York's shores with just seven flutes and a handful of dollars, he could hardly have imagined that his name would become synonymous with American wealth. Through shrewd business tactics and remarkable foresight, he built an empire in the fur trade that would lay the foundation for a fortune equivalent to billions in today's currency. [146,149,123] By his death in 1848, Astor had amassed $20 million – an unprecedented sum that made him America's first multi-millionaire and established a dynasty that would shape New York for generations. [147,145]

The transition of wealth to the second generation marked a crucial evolution in the family's fortune. William Backhouse Astor Sr., inheriting his father's real estate empire, demonstrated a different kind of business acumen. Under his stewardship, the family's holdings expanded dramatically through the development of commercial properties and residential buildings. By the time of his death in 1875, he had doubled the family fortune to nearly $50 million, [146,148,145] while also initiating the family's first major philanthropic ventures, including the establishment of the Astor Library. [146,147]

However, the true test of generational wealth came during the Gilded Age, when the family's fortune faced both unprecedented opportunities and challenges. The construction of the original Waldorf-Astoria Hotel complex perfectly illustrated these dynamics. Born from a family feud, when William Waldorf Astor demolished his father's mansion to spite his aunt Caroline, the hotel became a symbol of both family division and innovation. [150,125,142] The subsequent addition of the Astoria Hotel by John Jacob Astor IV created an unprecedented palace of luxury that revolutionized American hospitality.

Yet the tragic death of John Jacob Astor IV aboard the Titanic in 1912 marked a turning point in the family's fortunes. [146,145,150] As the twentieth century progressed, economic shifts and changing social dynamics began to erode the family's prominence. The Great Depression dealt a severe blow to their real estate holdings, forcing adaptations that previous generations hadn't faced. Vincent Astor, the last influential patriarch, recognized the need for change, selling portions of the family's properties and redirecting focus toward philanthropy through the Vincent Astor Foundation. [146,145,142]

Perhaps the most remarkable evolution came through Brooke Astor, Vincent's widow, who transformed the family's legacy from one of wealth accumulation to charitable distribution. Under her stewardship, the Vincent Astor Foundation supported numerous civic projects, from libraries and educational initiatives to public housing. Her efforts helped repair the family name, which had suffered from earlier generations' reputation for exploitation and harsh business practices. [149,145]

The evolution of the Astor fortune mirrors broader changes in American society's relationship with wealth and power. From John Jacob's monopolistic practices in the fur trade to Brooke's philanthropic endeavors, each generation adapted to changing social expectations and economic realities. [146,149,123] The family's journey from aggressive wealth accumulation to strategic philanthropy reflects America's own evolution in understanding the responsibilities that come with great fortune.

Today, as we witness new tech billionaires grappling with questions of wealth, responsibility, and legacy, the Astor story offers important lessons. Their experience demonstrates how generational wealth can either dissipate or transform, depending on each generation's ability to adapt to changing times. [145] The family's evolution from ruthless capitalists to civic benefactors established patterns of philanthropic giving that continue to influence modern charitable foundations and corporate social responsibility initiatives.

The lasting impact of this generational evolution extends beyond mere dollars and cents. The institutions they helped establish – from the New York Public Library to numerous cultural venues – continue to serve the public good, [146,147] while their story remains a compelling case study in how family fortunes can either adapt or decline across generations. In an era of growing wealth inequality and debate about the responsibilities of the ultra-wealthy, the Astor legacy offers both cautionary tales and inspiring examples of how great fortunes can be transformed into lasting public benefits. [145,142] The story of the Astor family stands as a testament to the transformative power of ambition, vision, and adaptability in American society. From John Jacob Astor's arrival as a penniless immigrant to the family's eventual reign over New York's social and cultural landscape, their journey embodies both the promise and paradox of the American Dream. Through strategic investments in Manhattan real estate, careful social engineering, and lasting contributions to the city's cultural institutions, the Astors helped shape not only the physical landscape of New York but also its social fabric in ways that continue to resonate today.

The family's evolution from merchants to social arbiters reflected broader changes in American society during the Gilded Age. Caroline Astor's creation of 'The Four Hundred' established patterns of social stratification that would influence American culture well beyond their era, while the family's architectural legacy – from the revolutionary Astor House to the magnificent Waldorf-Astoria – set new standards for American luxury and hospitality that persist to this day. Their philanthropy, though often serving dual purposes of civic improvement and social positioning, helped establish institutions that continue to enrich public life.

Yet perhaps the most enduring lesson of the Astor legacy lies in its demonstration of how private wealth can shape public culture, for better and worse. The contrast between their opulent lifestyle and the harsh conditions endured by the working class highlighted the deep social divisions of the Gilded Age – divisions that continue to echo in contemporary debates about wealth inequality and social responsibility. The transformation of their fortune across generations, from ruthless accumulation to strategic philanthropy, offers important insights for modern society as we grapple with questions about the role of private wealth in public life.

The parallels between the Gilded Age and our own era are striking. Just as the Astor's helped establish New York as a global capital of wealth and culture, today's tech billionaires and financial titans shape our cities and institutions. The social networks and exclusivity that Caroline Astor carefully cultivated find modern expression in private clubs, social media influence, and gated communities. Even the family's evolution toward philanthropy presaged contemporary discussions about the obligations of extreme wealth.

Today, as we witness growing wealth inequality and debate the responsibilities of the ultra-wealthy, the Astor story remains remarkably relevant. Their legacy lives on not only in the institutions they helped establish – from the New York Public Library to countless cultural venues – but also in the ongoing dialogue about wealth, power, and social responsibility in American society. As we face our own Gilded Age of technology billionaires and global capitalism, the Astor family's journey from immigrant merchants to social arbiters to philanthropists offers both cautionary tales and inspiring examples of how great fortunes can be transformed into lasting public benefits.

The physical landscape of modern Manhattan still bears the imprint of Astor influence, from the street names to the architectural standards they helped establish. More importantly, their story continues to illuminate the complex relationship between wealth, social status, and cultural influence that defines American society. As we look toward the future, the Astor legacy reminds us that the true measure of wealth lies not merely in its accumulation, but in how it shapes the world for generations to come.

Chapter Six

Newport's Summer Kings: The Social Battleground of America's Elite

In the summer of 1893, Alva Vanderbilt stood triumphantly on the marble terrace of Marble House, her newly completed Newport mansion that had cost a staggering $11 million to build – a testament to the extremes of Gilded Age excess. Below her stretched the manicured lawns leading to Bellevue Avenue, where a steady stream of carriages carried Newport's elite past her limestone palace, a building that would forever change the architectural landscape of America's premier summer resort. "One must always dress according to the occasion – even when there isn't one." - Alva Vanderbilt, 1895

The mansion would indeed become the crown jewel of Newport's already dazzling collection of summer "cottages," setting a new standard for architectural grandeur and social ambition in America's premier resort destination. Newport had transformed from a quiet colonial port into the ultimate arena where America's elite would wage their battles for social supremacy, using architecture, entertainment, and elaborate social rituals as their weapons of choice.

The transformation of Newport into the summer capital of American high society was no accident. As New York's wealthy families sought escape from the city's oppressive summer heat, Newport's cool ocean breezes and relative isolation made it the perfect stage for their social performances. The rocky coastline of Rhode Island became dotted with increasingly elaborate mansions, each designed to outshine its neighbors and assert its owner's place in the social hierarchy.

For these families, Newport represented more than just a summer retreat – it was a carefully cultivated social laboratory where the rules of elite society were written, tested, and enforced. Here, the distinction between old money and new became most pronounced, as established families like the Astors faced challenges from ambitious newcomers like the Vanderbilts, who used their immense industrial fortunes to buy their way into society's upper echelons.

Behind the glittering façade of Newport's social season lay a complex world of unwritten rules and ruthless social competition. Each dinner party, ball, and yacht race served as a battlefield where reputations could be made or destroyed. The summer of 1899 would prove to be particularly memorable, showcasing both the heights of Gilded Age excess and the growing tensions within American society.

The story of Mrs. Stuyvesant Fish's legendary dinner party at Beaulieu mansion captured the essence of Newport's extravagant summer season. Known for her razor-sharp wit and social daring, Mrs. Fish orchestrated an evening that would be talked about for generations. The centerpiece – a baby elephant borrowed from Barnum & Bailey's circus – perfectly symbolized the grandiose spectacle that Newport's social scene had become. Dining from golden plates while being entertained by circus performers, guests witnessed the ultimate expression of Gilded Age excess.

Yet this extraordinary display of wealth came at a time when many Americans were struggling through an economic depression. When questioned by a reporter about the lavish expenditure during such hard times, Mrs. Fish's infamous reply – "What else should we do with our money? Eat it?" – reflected the growing disconnect between America's elite and the rest of society. The incident became a lightning rod for public criticism, highlighting the increasing tensions between the nation's social classes.

This event, and countless others like it, contributed to the growing public fascination with – and resentment of – the super-wealthy's summer lifestyle. Newspapers across the country carried detailed accounts of Newport's social season, allowing average Americans to peek behind the curtain of elite society while simultaneously fueling calls for social reform and economic regulation.

In Newport's grand summer cottages, we find a microcosm of the Gilded Age itself – a world of unprecedented luxury and architectural achievement existing alongside growing social tensions and calls for change. The summer resort would continue to serve as America's most exclusive social stage, where the nation's elite would navigate the complex waters of class, culture, and wealth that would ultimately help shape modern American society.

The Rise of Newport: From Colonial Port to Summer Resort

"Newport represents the pinnacle of social aspiration in America – where even the wealthiest must prove themselves worthy of admission." - Mrs. Astor, 1883

On a misty morning in 1839, exactly two centuries after Newport's founding, a visiting merchant named Thomas Appleton stood at the harbor, lamenting the decline of what had once been colonial America's busiest port. The British occupation during the Revolution had devastated Newport's maritime trade, [154,155] leaving behind empty warehouses and quiet wharves where prosperity once reigned. Yet within those same weathered colonial buildings that had witnessed Newport's fall, the seeds of its remarkable transformation were already taking root.

Newport's journey from bustling colonial port to summer playground of America's elite was born of necessity and opportunity. As Providence claimed Rhode Island's industrial crown in the early 19th century, [154] Newport's business leaders and residents faced a crucial choice: fade into obscurity or reinvent their city. The answer came from an unexpected source – wealthy Southern planters seeking refuge from the oppressive summer heat. These early seasonal visitors discovered in Newport's cool ocean breezes and dramatic coastline the perfect escape from their plantation lives.

The city's colonial architecture, rather than being demolished for modern developments, became one of its greatest assets. The preserved historic homes and narrow streets offered an authenticity that appealed to wealthy visitors seeking to connect with America's past. The Redwood Library, founded in 1747, became a gathering place for intellectual discourse, attracting artists and writers like Henry James and Julia Ward Howe who helped establish Newport's reputation as a cultural haven. [154]

By the 1850s, Newport's transformation was accelerating. The arrival of the New York Yacht Club in 1844 marked a pivotal moment, bringing with it a wealthy clientele that would reshape the city's destiny. When William Shepard Wetmore built Chateau-sur-Mer in 1852, [152,153] it set a new standard for summer homes that would soon be eclipsed by even grander mansions. The modest "cottages" of the 1850s gave way to increasingly elaborate architectural statements, each designed to announce its owner's arrival in high society.

The contrast between old and new Newport was stark and telling. While the colonial section of town maintained its historic character, Bellevue Avenue emerged as a showcase of Gilded Age excess. [152,153,154] Local fishermen and tradespeople who had long called Newport home found themselves serving as gardeners, maids, and coachmen in the grand estates. The city became a living embodiment of America's widening class divisions, [151,154] where colonial simplicity and Gilded Age extravagance existed side by side.

The transformation reached its apex in the 1880s and 1890s, as America's industrial titans sought to outdo each other with ever more magnificent summer palaces. [152,153] Yet even as Newport became synonymous with wealth and social exclusivity, it retained traces of its maritime past. The fishermen's church bells still rang out on Sunday mornings, their sound carrying across the lawns of marble mansions to remind all of the city's humble beginnings.

This duality – between old and new, between working class and wealthy elite – would become Newport's defining characteristic. The city's evolution from colonial port to summer resort mirrors broader changes in American society during the Gilded Age: the shift from maritime trade to industrial wealth, from democratic simplicity to aristocratic pretension, from production to consumption. [154,156]

The legacy of this transformation continues to shape Newport and American society today. The preservation of both colonial buildings and Gilded Age mansions has made Newport a living museum of American architectural history. [152,153,154] The social patterns established during the resort era – the summer season, the debutante balls, the yacht races – influenced how wealth and status would be displayed throughout American society. Even the tension between old money and new, so evident in Newport's social battles, remains relevant in contemporary discussions of wealth and class in America. [154,156]

Perhaps most significantly, Newport's reinvention from declining port to premier resort demonstrated the power of American reinvention itself. Like many of the industrial titans who built their summer palaces there, Newport proved that a second act was possible in American life – if one had the vision, determination, and resources to achieve it. This lesson in adaptation and renewal would become a recurring theme in American urban development, as cities across the nation sought to reinvent themselves in the face of economic change.

Architectural Arms Race: The Building of Newport's 'Cottages'

"Architecture is frozen music." - William K. Vanderbilt, at the unveiling of Marble House, 1892

In the summer of 1892, as Alva Vanderbilt unveiled her magnificent Marble House to Newport society, she ignited what would become known as the greatest architectural arms race in American history. The mansion, requiring 500,000 cubic feet of marble and costing $11 million (equivalent to over $300 million today), set a new standard for opulence that would transform Newport's coastline and American architectural ambitions forever. [156,159]

The competition among America's wealthiest families to build increasingly grand "cottages" reflected deeper social currents of the Gilded Age. When Cornelius Vanderbilt II responded to his sister-in-law Alva's Marble House by commissioning The Breakers in 1893, he was doing more than simply building a summer home – he was making a statement about the Vanderbilt family's position at the pinnacle of American society. The 70-room Italian Renaissance-style palazzo, designed by architect Richard Morris Hunt, would become the grandest of all Newport cottages, [156,159] employing 2,000 workers and craftsmen during its construction.

The architectural ambitions of these families created an unprecedented demand for skilled labor. European craftsmen – stone carvers from Italy, woodworkers from France, plasterers from England – found themselves crossing the Atlantic to work on these magnificent projects. Local Newport laborers, too, found steady employment, though the contrast between their modest homes and the palaces they built was stark. One Irish stonemason working on The Breakers remarked to a reporter in 1894, "We're building castles for kings who weren't born royal."

Edward Berwind, the coal magnate, took the architectural competition in a different direction with The Elms in 1901. Rather than simply attempting to build the largest or most expensive mansion, Berwind focused on technological innovation. The Elms became one of the first fully electrified homes in America, featuring a sophisticated coal-fired electric plant in its basement. Its advanced ventilation system and early form of air conditioning demonstrated how new money could leverage modern technology to compete with old money's traditional grandeur. [160]

The interior decoration of these mansions became another battlefield for social competition. When Mrs. Oelrichs commissioned Allard and Sons of Paris to create the platinum-leafed panels for Rosecliff's ballroom in 1902, she was participating in a well-established pattern of cultural one-upmanship. Every detail, from the Baccarat crystal chandeliers to the hand-carved mahogany doors, served as a marker of taste and wealth. [157]

Yet beneath the gleaming marble facades lay a complex support system of servants and workers who made this lifestyle possible. The Breakers alone required a staff of 40 people to maintain it during the summer season. The servants' quarters, though well-appointed by working-class standards, offered a striking contrast to the opulence above. Hidden corridors and separate staircases kept servants largely invisible to the mansion's residents and guests, creating two parallel worlds within the same structure.

The architectural arms race reached its apex in the first decade of the 20th century. The construction of these summer palaces employed thousands, drove technological innovation, and set new standards for American architecture. [158,156] However, it also highlighted growing wealth inequality and social tensions. When the New York Times reported in 1904 that the combined cost of Newport's newest cottages exceeded the entire state budget of Rhode Island, it sparked public debate about the concentration of wealth in American society.

Today, these architectural masterpieces serve as museums and cultural institutions, preserved by the Preservation Society of Newport County. Their influence extends beyond their immediate era – the craftsmanship and architectural innovation they pioneered influenced American building practices for generations. The "cottages" of Newport remain powerful symbols of both the ambitions and excesses of the Gilded Age, [156,159] reminding us how the competitive spirit of America's industrial titans literally reshaped our architectural landscape.

The legacy of Newport's architectural arms race continues to influence modern American society. The relationship between wealth, architecture, and social status established during this period still resonates in contemporary discussions about luxury real estate and wealth inequality. The preservation of these mansions as public museums has democratized access to these once-exclusive spaces, while their maintenance challenges mirror broader debates about historical preservation versus modern development. [156] Perhaps most importantly, they stand as reminders of both the possibilities and responsibilities of great wealth in American society.

Social Warfare: Newport's Summer Season Rituals and Rules

"In society, one must remember that a closed door is worth a thousand words." - Caroline Astor, 1875

On a sweltering July evening in 1883, Caroline Astor stood at the entrance of her Newport villa, Beechwood, meticulously reviewing the guest list for that night's ball. Her legendary 'Four Hundred' – the definitive roster of New York and Newport society – would face its greatest test as new industrial wealth challenged old guard supremacy.

[163,164] The evening would crystallize the unwritten rules and ruthless social warfare that defined Newport's summer season.

The summer social season in Newport was far more than a series of parties – it was a carefully orchestrated battlefield where fortunes and reputations could be made or destroyed with a single invitation or snub. [154,163] Caroline Astor, alongside Ward McAllister, had established an intricate code of conduct that governed every aspect of social life, from the precise timing of afternoon calls to the exact number of courses appropriate for a dinner party. [161,154]

For the newly wealthy seeking entrance into this rarefied world, the path was treacherous. When the Vanderbilts first arrived in Newport, despite their enormous railroad fortune, they found themselves initially excluded from the most prestigious events. [154,163] Alva Vanderbilt's response – the legendary 1883 fancy dress ball at her New York mansion – demonstrated how new money could force its way into society through sheer spectacle and strategic social maneuvering. [165]

The daily rituals of Newport's summer season followed a precise schedule that served as the framework for social competition. Morning bathing at Bailey's Beach was restricted to an exclusive membership, with designated hours for swimming to ensure the 'right people' would encounter each other. [162] Afternoon coaching parades along Bellevue Avenue became elaborate displays of wealth, with families competing to showcase the finest horses and most elaborate carriages. [154]

Yet beneath the glittering surface of balls and yacht races lay a complex system of alliances and rivalries. The social calendar itself became a weapon, with competing hostesses deliberately scheduling overlapping events to force guests to choose sides. [154,163] When Mrs. Stuyvesant Fish hosted her famous dinner parties at Crossways, the guest list was scrutinized by all of Newport society for signs of shifting allegiances and social favor. [154]

The servants who maintained this world of luxury witnessed the intense social warfare from a unique vantage point. Mary O'Brien, a lady's maid at The Breakers, recorded in her diary how she would often work eighteen-hour days during the height of the season, preparing her mistress's elaborate costume changes while gathering intelligence about rival families from other servants. [163] The below-stairs network became an essential source of social information, as servants traded gossip that could make or break reputations.

The rules governing Newport society were both intricate and inflexible. Calling cards, for instance, followed a strict protocol – leaving one's card folded in specific ways conveyed different messages, and the timing of return calls was precisely calculated to demonstrate social standing. [161,154] Even the seemingly simple act of dining became a complex social performance, with elaborate place settings requiring up to 12 different forks and specific rules governing everything from wine selection to conversation topics. [154]

The ultimate arbiter of these social laws was the summer cottage itself. The architectural arms race among Newport's elite families created a hierarchy of entertainment spaces, with the grandest ballrooms and dining rooms conferring the power to host the season's most prestigious events. [154,165] When The Breakers was completed in 1895, its 70-room grandeur and 54-foot high Great Hall made it the undisputed stage for Newport's most coveted social invitations. [154,165]

However, this intense focus on social competition and display had consequences beyond Newport's gilded boundaries. The extreme concentration of wealth and its conspicuous display contributed to growing social tensions and calls for reform. [163] When news of Newport's lavish entertainments reached the public through newspaper accounts, it fueled progressive era critiques of inequality and excess.[163,165]

The legacy of Newport's social season continues to influence American society today. The complex rules and rituals established during the Gilded Age shaped modern American etiquette and social networking.[154,163] The tradition of strategic philanthropy, begun by Newport's summer residents seeking social advantage, evolved into contemporary models of charitable giving and social responsibility.[165] Even the concept of the 'summer season' as a time for networking and social positioning remains relevant in modern resort communities from the Hamptons to Aspen.

Most significantly, Newport's summer season established enduring patterns of social competition and display among America's elite.[154,163] The methods may have changed from calling cards to social media, but the fundamental dynamics of inclusion, exclusion, and social warfare through careful curation of one's social circle continue to shape American society. The summer cottages of Newport stand today as museums, but the social battles once fought within their walls offer enduring lessons about power, wealth, and the complex choreography of American high society.[154,163,165]

The Servants' World: Below Stairs in Newport's Mansions

"The measure of a great house is not in its marble halls, but in those who toil silently within its walls." - Ernest Birch, Butler to the Berwind family, 1901

In the pre-dawn darkness of a July morning in 1895, sixteen servants moved silently through the basement corridors of The Elms, Newport's newest architectural marvel.[166] As coal fires were stoked and kitchen ranges warmed, these essential workers began another exhausting seventeen-hour day [168] serving one of America's wealthiest families. Their world, hidden beneath the mansion's opulent facade, was one of endless stairs, strict hierarchies, and unwavering dedication to maintaining the illusion of effortless luxury above.

The contrast between upstairs and downstairs life at The Elms was stark and telling. While the Berwind family enjoyed their morning coffee served on Sèvres porcelain in sun-filled breakfast rooms, their servants had already been working for hours in the basement's artificial light. The French chef, commanding an unprecedented salary five times that of the butler, [167] orchestrated elaborate meal preparations in state-of-the-art kitchens. Meanwhile, maids and footmen navigated a complex network of hidden corridors and service stairs, designed to keep them invisible to the family and their guests. [167,169]

The servants' quarters on the third floor of The Elms told their own story of class distinction. Sixteen inside servants shared three bathrooms, their modest single-occupancy rooms a far cry from the luxurious chambers below. [169] Yet these accommodations, while sparse by upper-class standards, represented an improvement over typical working-class housing of the era. The Berwinds' British butler, Ernest Birch, maintained strict discipline among the staff, enforcing a rigid hierarchy that mirrored the social structure of the world above stairs. [166,167]

Technology played a crucial role in this hidden world. The Elms boasted one of Newport's first servant call systems – an elaborate network of bells and annunciator boxes that allowed family members to summon staff from any room. [166] This innovation eliminated the need for servants to wait constantly nearby, though it also meant they could be called upon at any moment, day or night. The basement's coal delivery system, featuring miniature railway tracks, demonstrated how industrial efficiency had been adapted to domestic service. [167,169]

The physical demands on servants were relentless. Laundry maids spent hours pressing the family's fine linens and delicate garments, while housemaids climbed countless stairs carrying coal scuttles and water pitchers. Even seemingly simple tasks, like preparing Mrs. Berwind's morning toilette, required multiple servants working in careful coordination. One former maid recalled having to iron shoelaces and place toothpaste on toothbrushes – small details that maintained the illusion of effortless elegance upstairs. [168,169]

Yet within this demanding environment, servants created their own community. The kitchen became a gathering place during brief moments of respite, where staff could share meals and exchange news about other households. The enclosed roof terraces, hidden from view by tall walls, offered rare opportunities for fresh air and relaxation during precious hours off. [167,169] These moments of camaraderie helped sustain workers through their grueling schedule of six-and-a-half-day weeks. [166]

The relationship between servants and their employers was complex. While the Berwinds maintained strict social boundaries, they also recognized exceptional service. Ernest Birch's decades of loyalty were ultimately rewarded with a substantial inheritance – an unusual acknowledgment for the era. [166] However, most servants remained anonymous figures in history, their contributions recorded only in household account books and staff registers. [167,169]

As the Gilded Age waned in the early twentieth century, this elaborate system of domestic service began to unravel. World War I created new opportunities for working-class Americans, while technological advances reduced the need for large household staffs. [168] The servant quarters at Newport's mansions gradually emptied, marking the end of an era when armies of workers sustained the lifestyles of America's elite.

Today, the preserved servants' quarters at mansions like The Elms offer a powerful reminder of the human cost of Gilded Age luxury. [169] The stories of these workers – their struggles, aspirations, and daily lives – provide crucial insight into class dynamics that continue to shape American society. While modern domestic service has evolved significantly, the fundamental questions about wealth, labor, and social mobility that emerged during the Gilded Age remain relevant in contemporary discussions about income inequality and workers' rights. The hidden world below stairs in Newport's mansions stands as a testament to both the grandeur and the complexity of America's past, reminding us that every great fortune rests upon the foundation of others' labor.

Newport's Preservation: From Private Estates to Public Museums

"The preservation of beauty is a sacred trust that we must pass on to future generations." - Doris Duke, 1958 [171]

On a crisp autumn morning in 1962, Katherine Warren stood before The Elms mansion, her heart heavy with the knowledge that this architectural masterpiece was slated for demolition. As president of the newly formed Preservation Society of Newport County, she faced what seemed an impossible task – raising enough funds to save this magnificent estate from the wrecking ball. [156,172] The mansion's contents had already been sold at auction, its rooms stripped bare of the opulent furnishings that once made it one of Newport's most celebrated homes.

The story of Newport's transformation from private pleasure palaces to public cultural treasures began in the wake of the Great Depression, when many of America's wealthiest families found themselves unable to maintain their massive summer "cottages." The Preservation Society of Newport County, founded in 1945, emerged as a crucial force in saving these architectural treasures. [170,159,156] Their first acquisition, Hunter House, a colonial-era mansion, marked the beginning of what would become one of America's most remarkable preservation efforts.

The turning point came in 1948 when the Preservation Society acquired The Breakers, the grandest of all Newport mansions, from Countess Gladys Széchenyi, daughter of Cornelius Vanderbilt II. This 70-room Italian Renaissance-style palazzo, which had cost $12 million to build in 1895 (equivalent to over $400 million today), became the cornerstone of Newport's preservation movement. [170,156] The Vanderbilt family's decision to ensure public access to The Breakers represented a significant shift in how America's elite viewed their architectural legacy.

When The Elms faced demolition in 1962, Katherine Warren and her colleagues launched an unprecedented campaign to save it. The mansion, built by coal magnate Edward Julius Berwind in 1901, represented the pinnacle of Gilded Age technological innovation, featuring one of America's first electric elevators and a sophisticated coal delivery system. [156,172] Through determined fundraising efforts and public advocacy, the Preservation Society succeeded in purchasing The Elms for $116,000 – a fraction of its original construction cost but a significant sum for a preservation organization in the 1960s.

The preservation of Marble House, another Vanderbilt mansion, revealed the complex motivations behind these conservation efforts. When Alva Vanderbilt's daughter Consuelo, the Duchess of Marlborough, sold the property in 1963, she insisted on conditions that would ensure its preservation and public accessibility. [159,172] This decision reflected a growing awareness among the descendants of Gilded Age families that their ancestral homes represented more than private wealth – they were vital pieces of American cultural heritage.

The transformation of these private estates into public museums required delicate balancing acts between historical authenticity and modern accessibility. When the Preservation Society began restoring The Elms in the 1960s, they faced the monumental task of recreating its original splendor. [156,172] Through painstaking research and the acquisition of period furnishings, they gradually brought the mansion back to life. The discovery of original furniture pieces at auctions and antique dealers became a kind of architectural treasure hunt, with each recovered item helping to tell the story of Gilded Age opulence.

Doris Duke's preservation of Rough Point represented a different approach to conservation. The tobacco heiress lived in the mansion until her death in 1993, simultaneously maintaining it as her private residence while preparing it for its future role as a museum. Her Newport Restoration Foundation, established in 1968, took on the broader mission of preserving Newport's architectural heritage, including many colonial-era buildings that predated the Gilded Age mansions. [171]

The preservation movement faced its share of challenges. The massive scale of these properties made maintenance costs astronomical. The Breakers alone required a full-time staff of specialists to maintain its 138,000 square feet of living space and 13 acres of grounds. [170,156] Yet innovative solutions emerged. The Preservation Society began hosting events in the mansions, from weddings at Rosecliff to flower shows in the gardens, creating new revenue streams while allowing public access to these magnificent spaces. [159]

Today, Newport's preserved mansions serve multiple roles: as museums documenting America's Gilded Age, as venues for cultural events, and as research centers for architectural and social historians. [170,159,156] The success of Newport's preservation movement has influenced similar efforts across the country, demonstrating how private wealth can be transformed into public cultural resources.

The legacy of this preservation effort extends far beyond Newport's shores. These mansions now serve as living laboratories where visitors can study the architecture, technology, and social customs of the Gilded Age. [170,156] The careful documentation of servant life in places like The Elms' restored basement has helped historians understand the complex social dynamics of the era. [159,172] Most importantly, these preserved estates remind us that the grandest private achievements can, through careful stewardship, become part of our shared cultural heritage.

The transformation of Newport's private mansions into public museums mirrors broader changes in American society – the democratization of cultural access, the recognition of architectural preservation as a public good, and the evolution of private wealth into public resources. [170,159,156] As modern America grapples with questions of wealth, inequality, and cultural heritage, Newport's preserved mansions stand as testament to how one era's private excesses can become another era's public treasures.

Cultural Legacy: Newport's Influence on American Society

"Society is like a lawn where every roughness is smoothed, every bramble eradicated, and where the eye is delighted by the smiling verdure of a velvet surface." - Caroline Astor, 1875

On a crisp September evening in 1883, as the last rays of summer sun glinted off the marble facades of Bellevue Avenue, Newport society gathered for what would become one of the most significant social events of the Gilded Age. Caroline Astor's annual end-of-season ball at Beechwood marked more than just another lavish celebration – it represented the culmination of Newport's transformation from colonial port town to America's premier social laboratory, where the rules of high society were written, tested, and eternally preserved. [163,156,170]

The influence of Newport's social season extended far beyond its manicured lawns and gilded ballrooms. Here, the complex dance between old money families like the Astors and new industrial wealth like the Vanderbilts created patterns of social interaction that would shape American society for generations. [156,170] When Alva Vanderbilt orchestrated her daughter Consuelo's debut at Marble House in 1895, she wasn't simply hosting a party – she was demonstrating how new money could use architectural grandeur and social spectacle to force their way into society's highest echelons. [170]

Newport's cultural impact manifested in multiple spheres, from architecture to social reform. The preservation of these summer "cottages" has provided an unparalleled window into Gilded Age aesthetics and values. [170,152] The Breakers, with its 70 rooms and Italian Renaissance inspiration, established new standards for American architectural ambition. [170] Meanwhile, The Elms showcased how industrial-age technology could be harnessed for domestic luxury, featuring one of America's first electric elevators and sophisticated coal delivery systems. [170]

Yet beneath the glittering surface of Newport society lay deeper currents of social change. The city's tradition of religious tolerance, dating back to its colonial founding, had fostered a unique environment where diverse communities could thrive. The Free African Union Society, established in 1780, demonstrated Newport's role as an early center of Black community organization and civil rights advocacy. [163,154] These parallel histories – of extreme wealth and grassroots activism – continue to influence discussions about social justice and economic inequality in America.

The intellectual and artistic legacy of Newport proved equally significant. The city attracted leading figures like Julia Ward Howe and William Ellery Channing, whose presence transformed summer gatherings into forums for discussing social reform, women's rights, and artistic innovation. [154,152] The Newport Art Museum, founded in 1912, emerged from this fertile cultural ground, establishing new models for how cultural institutions could serve both elite and public interests. [152]

Perhaps most significantly, Newport's summer season established enduring patterns of philanthropic giving and social responsibility among America's wealthy families. [156] When Caroline Astor hosted fundraising events for local charities at Beechwood, she set precedents for how social prominence could be leveraged for public benefit. The Preservation Society of Newport County's later success in saving these mansions from demolition demonstrated how private wealth could be transformed into public cultural resources. [152,170]

The influence of Newport's social season extended into the realm of fashion and etiquette, where the rules established during the Gilded Age continue to resonate. [156] The elaborate social rituals – from calling cards to dinner party protocols – codified by Mrs. Astor and Ward McAllister shaped American social customs far beyond Newport's shores. Even today, the "summer season" concept pioneered in Newport remains a feature of elite social life in resort communities across America. [156]

As modern America grapples with questions of wealth inequality, social mobility, and cultural preservation, Newport's legacy offers both cautionary tales and inspiring examples. The city's transformation from private pleasure ground to public cultural treasure demonstrates how societies can preserve their architectural and cultural heritage while making it accessible to all. [152,170] The complex social dynamics played out in Newport's mansions – between old and new money, between privilege and responsibility, between private luxury and public benefit – continue to inform contemporary debates about wealth, power, and social obligation in American society. [156,170]

Today, Newport's cultural influence lives on through its preserved mansions, thriving arts institutions, and enduring social traditions. [156,152,170] The city's journey from colonial port to Gilded Age resort to cultural landmark mirrors broader transformations in American society. As we face modern challenges of economic inequality and social justice, Newport's legacy reminds us that even the most exclusive spaces can, through careful stewardship and conscious choice, become part of our shared cultural heritage. As the sun set on Newport's Gilded Age supremacy in the early twentieth century, its influence on American society had already been indelibly etched into the nation's cultural fabric. The transformation of this quiet colonial port into the summer capital of American high society represented more than just a triumph of wealth and architectural ambition – it embodied the complex social dynamics that would shape modern America.

The story of Newport's summer cottages, from their construction to their preservation, mirrors broader themes in American history: the tension between old and new money, the relationship between private wealth and public benefit, and the evolution of American social institutions. When The Breakers opened its doors to the public in 1948, it marked a symbolic transition from private excess to public cultural heritage, demonstrating how even the most exclusive spaces could be transformed into shared national treasures.

The social warfare waged in Newport's ballrooms and along Bellevue Avenue established patterns of status and influence that continue to resonate in American society. The elaborate rituals and strict hierarchies of the summer season, though seemingly antiquated, laid the groundwork for modern social networking and status signaling. Even today's exclusive communities, from the Hamptons to Silicon Valley, echo Newport's complex interplay between established wealth and ambitious newcomers.

Perhaps most significantly, Newport's preservation movement demonstrated how private wealth could be channeled into public benefit. The transformation of these summer palaces into museums and cultural institutions set precedents for historic preservation and cultural stewardship that influence American society today. The work of organizations like the Preservation Society of Newport County showed how architectural heritage could be maintained while making it accessible to all.

The servant's world below stairs in Newport's mansions reminds us of the human cost of extreme wealth and the complex social structures that supported Gilded Age excess. Their stories, preserved in restored servants' quarters and household records, continue to inform discussions about labor, class, and social mobility in America. As modern society grapples with questions of wealth inequality and workers' rights, the experiences of Newport's service staff offer valuable historical perspective.

Today, Newport's summer cottages stand as more than just museums – they are living laboratories where we can study the dynamics of wealth, power, and social change in American society. The standards of luxury they established, the social practices they codified, and the architectural innovations they pioneered continue to influence American culture. From the design of modern luxury homes to the protocols of high society events, Newport's legacy endures.

As we reflect on Newport's influence on modern America, we see how the social experiments conducted in this seaside resort shaped national patterns of wealth display, cultural philanthropy, and social mobility. The tension between exclusivity and accessibility, private wealth and public benefit, individual ambition and social responsibility – all these themes played out in Newport's grand mansions continue to resonate in contemporary American society.

The preservation of Newport's architectural heritage serves as both inspiration and warning – a reminder of the possibilities and perils of concentrated wealth, the importance of cultural stewardship, and the enduring American struggle to balance individual achievement with social responsibility. In the end, Newport's transformation from private pleasure ground to public cultural treasure offers valuable lessons for modern society as we navigate our own questions of wealth, power, and social obligation.

Chapter Seven

Philanthropy and Power: How Gilded Age Fortunes Built Modern America

On a October morning in 1902, Andrew Carnegie stood before the newly completed Carnegie Institute of Technology in Pittsburgh, his $2 million gift to the city where he had built his fortune. 'The man who dies thus rich, dies disgraced,' he declared, embodying his Gospel of Wealth philosophy that would inspire generations of philanthropists and fundamentally reshape American institutional life. His words that day would echo through American history, fundamentally reshaping how society viewed the responsibilities of wealth. The rise of strategic philanthropy during the Gilded Age marked a transformative shift in how America's industrial fortunes would shape the nation's future. The wealthy elite, having amassed unprecedented fortunes through industry and finance, began to grapple with a pressing question: what obligation did they have to society?

The founding of the University of Chicago stands as perhaps the most striking example of this new approach to philanthropic giving. When Baptist leaders approached John D. Rockefeller in 1890 about establishing a new university in Chicago, the opportunity perfectly aligned with his vision for strategic giving. Rockefeller had long believed that education was the key to social progress, but he was determined to move beyond traditional charitable giving to create lasting institutional change.

His initial gift of $600,000 came with unprecedented conditions that would revolutionize philanthropic practice. The Baptist Education Society would need to raise matching funds from other donors – a novel concept at the time that forced institutions to develop sustainable funding models rather than rely solely on wealthy patrons. This approach sparked what would become one of the most successful early fundraising campaigns in American education, with Chicago's business leaders and citizens ultimately contributing over $1 million to match Rockefeller's challenge.

When the University of Chicago opened its doors in October 1892, it represented far more than just another institution of higher learning. Its very structure – combining German-style research emphasis with American practical innovation – embodied a new vision for education in America. Rockefeller's total contribution would eventually exceed $35 million (equivalent to nearly a billion dollars today), but the true revolution lay in his approach to giving. By demanding matching funds, insisting on professional management, and focusing on measurable results, Rockefeller established patterns of strategic philanthropy that continue to influence charitable giving in the modern era.

The University of Chicago's founding marked a crucial transition from traditional charitable giving to modern institutional philanthropy. No longer was philanthropy simply about alleviating immediate needs – it had become a tool for creating lasting social change through carefully structured institutions. This new model would be replicated countless times as America's industrial titans sought to transform their vast fortunes into engines of social progress.

Yet beneath these grand gestures lay complex motivations that speak to the very heart of the Gilded Age. While men like Rockefeller genuinely believed in the transformative power of education and research, their philanthropic efforts also served to legitimize their vast fortunes in an era of growing social unrest. The creation of universities, libraries, and cultural institutions helped reshape public perception of industrial wealth, suggesting that great fortunes could serve great purposes.

As we explore the landscape of Gilded Age philanthropy in this chapter, we'll see how America's wealthiest families used their fortunes to build institutions that continue to shape our society today. From Carnegie's libraries to Morgan's museums, from Rockefeller's universities to Vanderbilt's hospitals, these philanthropic ventures tell a complex story of ambition, obligation, and lasting legacy. They remind us that the relationship between wealth and social responsibility remains as relevant today as it was in the Gilded Age, perhaps even more so in our current era of growing wealth inequality.

The Gospel of Wealth: Carnegie's Philosophy of Strategic Giving

"The problem of our age is the proper administration of wealth, so that the ties of brotherhood may still bind together the rich and poor in harmonious relationship." These words, penned by Andrew Carnegie in his 1889 essay 'The Gospel of Wealth,' [173,74] would fundamentally reshape how America's wealthiest citizens viewed their obligations to society. Carnegie wasn't just theorizing – he would go on to give away the equivalent of over $65 billion in today's money, establishing thousands of libraries, schools, and cultural institutions across America. [173,176]

On a cold December morning in 1889, Carnegie stood before the assembled trustees of the Cooper Union in New York City, defending his controversial new philosophy about wealth. The occasion marked his first public address about 'The Gospel of Wealth,' and the audience included both admirers and skeptics. Among them sat several of his fellow industrialists, uncomfortable with Carnegie's assertion that the wealthy were mere 'trustees' of their fortunes, morally obligated to use their money for the public good. [173,74,176]

Carnegie's philosophy represented a radical departure from traditional charitable giving. He firmly rejected what he called 'indiscriminate almsgiving,' arguing instead for strategic philanthropy that would create lasting opportunities for self-improvement. [173,177] 'In bestowing charity,' he declared that day, 'the main consideration should be to help those who will help themselves.' This wasn't just theoretical posturing – Carnegie had already begun implementing his philosophy through the systematic establishment of public libraries across America. [173,176]

The contrast between Carnegie's opulent lifestyle and his philanthropic mission created fascinating tensions. While he preached about the obligations of wealth, he lived in a magnificent mansion on Fifth Avenue and spent summers in his Scottish castle, Skibo. Yet unlike many of his peers, Carnegie viewed this wealth as a temporary trust rather than a permanent possession. He famously declared that 'the man who dies thus rich, dies disgraced,' and he meant it – by the time of his death in 1919, he had given away nearly 90% of his fortune. [173,177,74]

Carnegie's strategic approach to giving transformed American philanthropy. When establishing his libraries, he insisted that local communities provide the land and commit to ongoing maintenance through public funding. [173,176] This matching requirement ensured community buy-in and long-term sustainability. In Braddock, Pennsylvania, where one of his first libraries was established, the local steel workers initially viewed the library with suspicion – another top-down initiative from their wealthy employer. However, the library's impact proved transformative, providing generations of workers and their children with access to education and self-improvement. [176]

The implementation of Carnegie's philosophy wasn't without its critics. Labor leaders pointed out the irony of a man who had amassed his fortune through harsh labor practices now positioning himself as a public benefactor. During the infamous Homestead Strike of 1892, workers at Carnegie's steel mills questioned how their employer could reconcile his philanthropic ideals with the violent suppression of labor unions. [84] These contradictions highlighted the complex relationship between industrial wealth and social responsibility in the Gilded Age. [84,177]

Yet Carnegie's influence extended far beyond his era. His emphasis on strategic giving and measurable outcomes revolutionized philanthropic practice. [174,176] The creation of the Carnegie Corporation in 1911, with its professional management and focused mission, established a model for modern charitable foundations. [174,175] Today's major philanthropists, from Bill Gates to MacKenzie Scott, echo Carnegie's philosophy of giving while living and focusing on systemic change rather than mere charity. [173]

The Gospel of Wealth's legacy continues to shape contemporary debates about wealth inequality and social responsibility. As modern billionaires grapple with questions of philanthropic obligation, Carnegie's central insight – that extreme wealth carries moral obligations to society – remains powerfully relevant. [173,74] His vision of strategic philanthropy, focused on creating opportunities for self-improvement rather than mere handouts, continues to influence how we think about addressing social challenges through private wealth. [173,177]

In many ways, Carnegie's philosophy represented both the best and worst of the Gilded Age – a genuine commitment to social progress combined with a paternalistic belief in the superior wisdom of the wealthy. [84] Yet his lasting impact on American institutions, from the thousands of Carnegie libraries that still dot the American landscape to the ongoing work of the Carnegie Corporation, demonstrates how one man's philosophy about wealth and responsibility helped shape modern American society. [173,176]

Educational Empires: Universities and Libraries of the Gilded Age

"The man who dies rich, dies disgraced." - Andrew Carnegie's words echoed through the marble halls of America's newest libraries and universities, institutions that would forever transform the nation's educational landscape. On a crisp autumn morning in 1891, as the University of Chicago's first buildings rose from the Illinois prairie, John D. Rockefeller stood contemplating his most ambitious philanthropic venture yet. The oil magnate had already committed $600,000 to the project, but this was just the beginning of what would become a $35 million investment in higher education. [38]

The creation of these educational empires marked a dramatic shift in American intellectual life. In the span of just three decades, from 1870 to 1900, the landscape of American education was transformed by the unprecedented wealth of the Gilded Age. Libraries and universities sprouted across the nation, funded by fortunes built on oil, steel, and railroads. Yet behind these grand facades lay complex motivations – a mixture of genuine altruism, social ambition, and the desire to shape American society. [179,38]

Consider the remarkable story of Andrew Carnegie's library campaign. Between 1886 and 1919, Carnegie funded 1,679 public libraries across America, investing over $40 million in what he called 'the best ladder upon which the aspiring can rise.' Each grant came with strict conditions – communities had to provide the land and commit to maintaining the libraries through public funding. [178,179] In Braddock, Pennsylvania, where Carnegie built one of his first libraries, the steel workers who labored in his mills initially viewed the project with skepticism. Yet over time, these libraries became transformative institutions, providing generations of working-class Americans with access to knowledge previously reserved for the wealthy. [179,181]

The University of Chicago's founding revealed another dimension of Gilded Age educational philanthropy. Rockefeller's involvement went far beyond mere funding – he insisted on professional management and measurable results, establishing patterns that would influence institutional philanthropy for generations. When Baptist leaders first approached him about establishing the university, Rockefeller seized the opportunity to create something unprecedented: a research institution that would rival the ancient universities of the East while embracing modern scientific methods. [38]

The contrast between these philanthropic endeavors and the broader social context was stark. While Carnegie was building libraries, his steel workers in Homestead worked twelve-hour days in dangerous conditions. While Rockefeller was funding universities, his Standard Oil Company was crushing competitors and manipulating markets. This paradox lay at the heart of Gilded Age philanthropy – the same fortunes that created unprecedented inequality also funded institutions that would help democratize knowledge and opportunity. [179,38]

Cornelius Vanderbilt's 1873 gift of $1 million to establish Vanderbilt University in Nashville represented yet another approach to educational philanthropy. The Commodore, who had never shown much interest in education during his lifetime, made this donation near the end of his life. The gift was intended to help heal the wounds of the Civil War by providing quality education in the South, though it also served to cement Vanderbilt's legacy in a region where his railroad empire held significant influence. [180]

These educational empires reshaped not just American education but American society itself. Carnegie's libraries democratized access to knowledge in ways previously unimaginable. By 1919, nearly half of all American public libraries were Carnegie libraries, their distinctive architecture becoming symbols of civic pride and cultural aspiration. [179,181] The research universities established during this period – Chicago, Stanford, and others – helped transform American higher education from a classical model focused on character development to one emphasizing research and practical knowledge. [38]

The legacy of these educational empires continues to shape American society today. The modern research university, with its emphasis on both pure research and practical application, emerged from this period. The public library system, now a cornerstone of American democracy, was fundamentally shaped by Carnegie's vision. [178,179] Even the basic concept of strategic philanthropy – with its emphasis on sustainability, matching funds, and measurable outcomes – emerged from these Gilded Age experiments in educational giving [179]

Yet perhaps the most profound legacy lies in how these institutions helped democratize opportunity in American society. While the fortunes that built them were often accumulated through practices we now consider problematic, the libraries and universities they created helped provide generations of Americans with tools for social mobility and intellectual growth. [178,181] In this way, the educational empires of the Gilded Age embody both the contradictions of their era and the enduring American belief in education as a path to opportunity.

Medical Innovation: Rockefeller Institute and Modern Healthcare

"The best philanthropy is constantly in search of the finalities – a search for a cause, an attempt to cure evils at their source." - John D. Rockefeller Sr.'s words echoed through the marble halls of the newly established Rockefeller Institute for Medical Research in 1901. Standing before the Institute's first laboratory building on York Avenue in Manhattan, Rockefeller contemplated how personal tragedy had led to this moment. The death of his grandson from scarlet fever had deeply affected him, sparking a revolution in American medical research that would transform healthcare forever. [182,183,184]

On a crisp autumn morning in 1901, Frederick T. Gates, Rockefeller's trusted advisor, stood beside him as they watched researchers file into the nation's first biomedical research institute. [182,185] Gates had convinced Rockefeller that systematic scientific research could seek to understand and eliminate the root causes of disease. [183] The Institute represented a radical departure from traditional charitable giving – instead of simply treating the sick, it would seek to understand and eliminate the root causes of disease.

The contrast between the Institute's pristine laboratories and the crowded tenements just blocks away was stark. While researchers worked with cutting-edge equipment in well-ventilated rooms, the poor of New York's Lower East Side struggled with tuberculosis, diphtheria, and typhoid fever in cramped, unsanitary conditions. [182,183,184] This juxtaposition embodied both the promise and the paradox of Gilded Age philanthropy – immense wealth funding scientific progress while basic public health challenges persisted.

In 1910, the addition of the Rockefeller University Hospital marked a revolutionary step forward. As the first American hospital dedicated exclusively to clinical research, it bridged the gap between laboratory science and patient care. [182,183,184] Dr. Simon Flexner, the Institute's first director, insisted on a novel approach – researchers would move freely between laboratory benches and hospital beds, ensuring that scientific discoveries translated directly into improved treatments. [182,185]

The Institute's early achievements were remarkable. Under Flexner's leadership, researchers developed an innovative delivery system for anti-meningitis serum, dramatically reducing mortality rates. [182,185] Dr. Hideyo Noguchi made groundbreaking discoveries about syphilis, while Dr. Louise Pearce and her colleagues developed the first effective treatment for African sleeping sickness. Perhaps most significantly, Dr. Peyton Rous discovered that certain cancers could be caused by viruses, a finding so revolutionary that it was initially dismissed by the medical establishment. [182]

By 1940, the Institute's influence had transformed American medicine. Nearly half of the leading positions in U.S. academic internal medicine were held by alumni of the Rockefeller Hospital's training programs. [183,185] The Institute's emphasis on rigorous laboratory research combined with clinical observation became the model for medical education nationwide. When Oswald Avery and his colleagues demonstrated that DNA carries genetic information in 1944, they fundamentally reshaped our understanding of life itself. [183,185]

The Institute's legacy extends far beyond its scientific breakthroughs. It established a new model of strategic philanthropy, where immense wealth could be systematically applied to solve fundamental societal challenges. This approach influenced subsequent philanthropic efforts, from the Gates Foundation to modern medical research funding. Today, as we face global health challenges like COVID-19, the Institute's pioneering integration of laboratory research with clinical practice remains more relevant than ever. 185

The story of the Rockefeller Institute embodies the complex dynamics of Gilded Age philanthropy – how personal tragedy could inspire systematic change, how immense wealth could be transformed into public good, and how scientific progress could coexist with persistent social inequality. As we grapple with contemporary healthcare challenges and debates about wealth inequality, the Institute's history offers both inspiration and caution, reminding us that transformative change requires not just resources, but vision, strategy, and a commitment to addressing problems at their root.

Cultural Patronage: Museums, Opera Houses, and the Arts

"Art is the soul of life and the doorway to experience." These words, spoken by J.P. Morgan in 1902, captured the spirit of cultural ambition that drove the Gilded Age's most ambitious artistic endeavors. On an autumn evening in 1883, the newly constructed Metropolitan Opera House blazed with light as New York's elite gathered for its inaugural performance. The massive building, funded by seventy prominent families including the Vanderbilts, Morgans, and Goulds, stood as a direct challenge to the old-money stronghold of the Academy of Music, where the Astors and their circle had long controlled access to high culture through their monopoly on opera boxes. [187]

The "War of the Operas," as it came to be known, perfectly exemplified how cultural patronage became a battlefield for social supremacy in Gilded Age New York. The Academy of Music, with its mere eighteen premium boxes, had become a powerful tool for social exclusion. When the nouveau riche were denied access to these coveted spaces, they responded with characteristic boldness – building their own opera house with 122 boxes, effectively democratizing elite cultural spaces while simultaneously creating new hierarchies of privilege. [187,188]

J.P. Morgan's involvement with the Metropolitan Museum of Art revealed another dimension of cultural patronage. As one of the museum's principal benefactors, Morgan transformed the institution through his extraordinary collecting activities and financial support. [18] His personal collection, valued at over $60 million (equivalent to billions today), included masterpieces that would form the cornerstone of the museum's European collections. Yet Morgan's patronage went beyond mere collecting – he understood that cultural institutions could serve as powerful instruments of social legitimacy and civic pride. [55,18]

The contrast between these glittering temples of culture and the reality of working-class life was stark. While the elite debated the merits of Wagner versus Verdi in their velvet-lined boxes, just blocks away in the tenements of the Lower East Side, immigrants crowded into squalid conditions, their children working in factories rather than attending concerts. This disparity was not lost on contemporary observers – newspapers of the era frequently commented on the irony of industrial fortunes funding high culture while industrial workers struggled for basic necessities.

Yet the impact of this cultural patronage would extend far beyond the Gilded Age elite's social ambitions. The Metropolitan Museum of Art, established in 1870, exemplified the era's complex marriage of private wealth and public benefit. [18] While the museum's founding trustees were drawn from New York's wealthiest families, they established an institution that would eventually become one of the world's great public art collections. The museum's charter explicitly required it to be open to the public free of charge several days each week, a radical concept for its time.

The Boston Museum of Fine Arts, founded the same year, reflected similar dynamics. Boston's elite families, determined to establish their city as a cultural capital, created an institution that would both display their refined tastes and serve as an educational resource for the broader public. [189] The museum's early focus on European masterworks reflected the cultural aspirations of its patrons, who sought to transplant Old World sophistication to New World soil.

These cultural institutions served multiple purposes – they were simultaneously monuments to private wealth, instruments of social control, and engines of public education. [189] The Metropolitan Opera House, for instance, while built as a symbol of new money's cultural aspirations, would eventually become one of the world's premier venues for performing arts, accessible to a far broader audience than its founders might have envisioned.

The legacy of this cultural patronage continues to shape American society today. The institutions established during the Gilded Age – from Carnegie Hall to the Metropolitan Museum – remain cornerstones of American cultural life. [186,18] Their founding paradox - private wealth serving public benefit – continues to influence how we fund and manage cultural institutions. The modern museum, with its dual mission of preserving elite culture while making it accessible to the public, emerged directly from this era's complex negotiations between exclusivity and accessibility.

Moreover, the pattern of cultural philanthropy established during the Gilded Age – wealthy patrons funding institutions that serve the public good – remains a distinctively American approach to supporting the arts. Today's cultural institutions still depend heavily on private philanthropy, a model that sets them apart from their more state-funded European counterparts. This reliance on private support, with its attendant tensions between donor influence and public benefit, is perhaps the most enduring legacy of Gilded Age cultural patronage.

Religious and Social Reform: Faith-Based Philanthropy

"The Gospel of Jesus Christ is the only force in the world that is genuinely changing society," declared Dwight L. Moody to a packed audience at his Chicago revival meeting in 1876. [192] Standing before thousands of eager listeners, the renowned evangelist articulated a vision of faith-based reform that would help reshape American society during the Gilded Age. As industrial fortunes created unprecedented wealth alongside grinding poverty, religious leaders and wealthy philanthropists sought to address social challenges through a distinctively American blend of faith and charity.

In 1877, Moody's revival meetings drew both wealthy industrialists and desperate laborers to Chicago's Farwell Hall. [192] The evangelist's message of personal salvation and social responsibility resonated across class lines, offering hope to the downtrodden while challenging the wealthy to use their resources for moral purposes. [192] These revival meetings became a powerful catalyst for faith-based philanthropy, inspiring wealthy attendees to fund numerous charitable initiatives while encouraging working-class participants to embrace temperance and self-improvement.

The Social Gospel movement emerged as perhaps the most influential religious response to Gilded Age inequalities. Protestant leaders, deeply troubled by urban poverty and social disorder, began arguing that Christian faith demanded direct engagement with societal problems. [190,191] They viewed industrialization's human costs – child labor, dangerous working conditions, overcrowded tenements – as moral challenges requiring both individual charity and systematic reform.

The contrast between religious ideals and social realities was stark. While Cornelius Vanderbilt attended elaborate church services in his private chapel, immigrant families crowded into squalid tenements just blocks away. This disparity troubled many religious leaders, who began questioning whether traditional charity was sufficient to address industrial society's challenges. The Social Gospel movement's answer was clear – Christians had a moral obligation to transform society itself, not merely assist individual sufferers. [190]

Marie Herbert, a prominent voice in the movement, insisted that scripture provided not just spiritual guidance but a blueprint for social justice. [191] Speaking at a gathering of Protestant reformers in 1885, she declared, 'The Bible demands we build a just society, not merely console ourselves with promises of heaven while ignoring hell on earth.' Her words captured the movement's revolutionary implications – faith required confronting systemic inequalities, not just individual sins. [191]

The Women's Christian Temperance Union (WCTU) exemplified how faith-based reform efforts could transcend traditional charitable activities. [18] Under the leadership of Frances Willard, the organization expanded beyond its initial focus on alcohol to address women's rights, labor conditions, and public health. The WCTU's evolution demonstrated how religious conviction could fuel broader social reform movements, though its middle-class Protestant values sometimes created tensions with immigrant and working-class communities. [192]

Settlement houses represented another crucial intersection of faith and social reform. While not exclusively religious institutions, many were founded and staffed by individuals deeply influenced by Social Gospel teachings. [190] These urban outposts provided education, healthcare, and social services while attempting to bridge class divides through direct engagement between middle-class reformers and poor communities.

The legacy of Gilded Age faith-based philanthropy continues to shape American society. Modern non-profit organizations, social welfare programs, and debates about wealth's moral obligations all reflect patterns established during this era. [190] The complex relationship between religious conviction and social reform – sometimes complementary, sometimes contradictory – remains central to American discussions about poverty, inequality, and social justice.

Today's faith-based initiatives, whether focused on homelessness, addiction recovery, or educational opportunity, build on foundations laid during the Gilded Age. [19] The period's distinctive blend of personal salvation and social transformation, of individual charity and systematic reform, continues to influence how Americans approach societal challenges. As we grapple with contemporary inequalities, the successes and limitations of Gilded Age faith-based philanthropy offer crucial lessons about the possibilities and pitfalls of using religious conviction to drive social change.

Legacy Building: The Creation of Charitable Foundations

"The man who dies rich, dies disgraced." These words, penned by Andrew Carnegie in his seminal 1889 essay 'The Gospel of Wealth,' [193,196] would fundamentally reshape how America's wealthiest citizens approached philanthropy. On a crisp autumn morning in 1911, Carnegie stood before the newly established Carnegie Corporation of New York, his $135 million endowment (equivalent to several billion today) representing the culmination of his philanthropic vision. [193]

The moment marked a revolutionary shift in how America's industrial fortunes would be channeled toward social progress.

The creation of modern charitable foundations during the Gilded Age emerged from a complex web of motivations – genuine altruism, social pressure, and the desire to shape society according to the donors' visions. [193,55] In 1913, when John D. Rockefeller signed the documents establishing the Rockefeller Foundation with an initial gift of $100 million, [193,55,197] he was creating more than just another charitable organization. This new institution would pioneer systematic approaches to philanthropy that continue to influence giving today.

The contrast between these grand philanthropic gestures and the social conditions that spawned them was stark. While Rockefeller was endowing his foundation in his mansion on 54th Street, just miles away in the tenements of the Lower East Side, immigrants worked fourteen-hour days in sweatshops, their children lacking basic education and healthcare. [55,18] This paradox – immense wealth funding social progress while the conditions that created that wealth remained unchanged – lay at the heart of Gilded Age philanthropy.

The establishment of these foundations marked a crucial shift from traditional charitable giving to strategic philanthropy. When the Rockefeller Foundation launched its first major initiative – a campaign to eradicate hookworm disease in the American South [193,197] – it demonstrated how systematic research and coordinated action could address social problems at their root. The foundation's work combined scientific expertise with business efficiency, establishing patterns that would influence philanthropic practice for generations.

Carnegie's approach to foundation-building reflected his systematic mindset. Rather than simply distributing wealth, he created specialized organizations for specific purposes – the Carnegie Institution of Washington for scientific research, the Carnegie Foundation for the

Advancement of Teaching for educational reform, and the Carnegie Corporation as an overarching philanthropic body. [193,196] Each institution operated with clear objectives and professional management, transforming charitable giving from an ad hoc practice into a structured enterprise.

The impact of these early foundations extended far beyond their immediate programs. When the General Education Board, established by Rockefeller in 1902, began supporting African American education in the South, [193,195] it helped lay the groundwork for future civil rights advances. Similarly, the Rockefeller Foundation's support for medical research and public health initiatives helped establish the infrastructure for modern global health programs. [193,197]

Yet these foundations also faced significant criticism. During the 1915 Congressional hearings on industrial relations, Chairman Frank Walsh accused the Rockefeller Foundation of being 'an institution designed to perpetuate the present position of predatory wealth.' [194,196] This criticism highlighted growing public concern about the influence of private wealth over public institutions – a debate that continues today.

The legacy of these Gilded Age foundations remains visible in contemporary America. The models they established – professional management, strategic focus, emphasis on research and measurable outcomes – continue to influence modern philanthropic organizations from the Gates Foundation to the Ford Foundation. [193,197] Their successes and failures offer crucial lessons about the possibilities and limitations of using private wealth to address public challenges.

As we grapple with modern questions about wealth inequality and social responsibility, the story of these early foundations remains remarkably relevant. Their creation marked a pivotal moment when America's industrial fortunes were first systematically directed toward public benefit, [193,55] establishing patterns of philanthropic giving that continue to shape our society. The tensions they navigated – between private wealth and public good, between charitable relief and systematic reform, between donor control and public accountability [194,196] – remain at the heart of contemporary debates about philanthropy's role in American society.

The establishment of these foundations also represented a crucial shift in how wealth was viewed in American society. Rather than simply passing fortunes to the next generation, these industrialists chose to create institutions that would outlive them, working to address social challenges in perpetuity. [193,195] This new model of philanthropy helped legitimize the accumulation of great wealth while establishing expectations about the social responsibilities that came with it – expectations that continue to influence public attitudes toward wealth and giving in modern America. As we reflect on the transformative power of Gilded Age philanthropy, we are reminded of Andrew Carnegie's prescient observation that 'wealth is not to feed our pride but to feed the poor.' The grand philanthropic endeavors of this era – from Carnegie's libraries to Rockefeller's universities, from Morgan's museums to Vanderbilt's medical institutions – fundamentally reshaped American society in ways that continue to influence us today.

The creation of modern philanthropic foundations marked a pivotal shift in how society viewed the responsibilities of wealth. When John D. Rockefeller established the Rockefeller Foundation in 1913, he wasn't just creating another charitable organization – he was pioneering a new model of strategic giving that would transform how private wealth could be leveraged for public benefit. The foundation's early work in public health, including its successful campaign against hookworm disease in the American South, demonstrated how systematic research and coordinated action could address social problems at their root.

Yet this era's philanthropy was marked by profound contradictions. While Carnegie built libraries to democratize knowledge, his steel workers labored under harsh conditions in Homestead. As Rockefeller funded groundbreaking medical research at his institute, immigrant families crowded into tenements just blocks away. These paradoxes remind us that the relationship between private wealth and public good has always been complex, shaped by both genuine altruism and the desire for social legitimacy.

The cultural institutions established during this period – from the Metropolitan Museum of Art to the Metropolitan Opera – remain cornerstones of American cultural life. Through J.P. Morgan's art collecting and the Vanderbilts' patronage of music, these wealthy families helped establish New York as a global cultural capital. Yet even these artistic endeavors reflected the era's social tensions, as evidenced by the 'War of the Operas' between old and new money families.

The legacy of Gilded Age philanthropy extends far beyond the institutions it created. The model of strategic giving pioneered by these industrial titans – with its emphasis on research, measurable outcomes, and systematic change – continues to influence modern philanthropic practice. From the Gates Foundation to the Chan Zuckerberg Initiative, today's major philanthropic organizations build upon patterns established during the Gilded Age.

Perhaps most significantly, this era's philanthropy helped establish enduring expectations about the social responsibilities of wealth. The idea that great fortunes carry moral obligations to society, so powerfully articulated in Carnegie's 'Gospel of Wealth,' remains a powerful force in American culture. As we grapple with contemporary questions about wealth inequality and social responsibility, the successes and failures of Gilded Age philanthropy offer crucial lessons about how private wealth can be mobilized for public benefit.

Looking forward, the challenges that inspired Gilded Age philanthropy – educational access, public health, cultural development, and social mobility – remain remarkably relevant. While the specific manifestations of these challenges have evolved, the fundamental questions about how society should balance private wealth with public good continue to shape our national dialogue. In this way, the philanthropic innovations of the Gilded Age not only transformed their own era but continue to influence how we approach social change in modern America.

Conclusion

As we reflect on the transformative era of the Gilded Age and its towering figures, we see how their legacies continue to shape modern America. The architectural marvels they built still dominate our skylines, from Grand Central Terminal to the Metropolitan Museum of Art. Their philanthropic institutions – Carnegie's libraries, Rockefeller's universities, Morgan's cultural foundations – remain vital centers of learning and culture. Yet their most enduring impact may be the economic and social structures they helped create, for better or worse.

These titans of industry reshaped not just New York but the very fabric of American capitalism. Vanderbilt's railroad consolidations established patterns of corporate organization that persist today. Rockefeller's Standard Oil innovations in vertical integration and management structure became blueprints for modern multinational corporations. Morgan's financial methods laid the groundwork for Wall Street's continued dominance of global markets. The Astors' real estate empire demonstrated how generational wealth could be preserved and multiplied through strategic property investment.

The social structures they created proved equally influential. Caroline Astor's rigid codification of society's upper echelons evolved into today's complex status hierarchies. The lavish displays of Newport's summer season presaged our modern celebrity culture. Their philanthropic innovations – from Carnegie's systematic giving to Rockefeller's scientific approach to charity – transformed how wealth could be deployed for social benefit, establishing patterns that today's billionaires still follow.

Yet the Gilded Age also left us with challenging questions that remain unresolved. The tension between private wealth and public good, so evident in Morgan's role as an unofficial central banker, continues to spark debate about financial regulation. The labor conflicts at Homestead and elsewhere laid bare contradictions between American ideals of opportunity and the realities of industrial capitalism. The extreme inequality of the era finds echoes in today's discussions about wealth concentration and social responsibility.

Perhaps most significantly, these figures embodied fundamental American contradictions – between democracy and plutocracy, between free markets and monopoly power, between private ambition and public benefit. Rockefeller's ruthless business tactics coexisted with genuine philanthropic conviction. Carnegie's brutal labor practices occurred alongside sincere efforts to spread knowledge through his libraries. These complexities remind us that simple moral judgments rarely capture historical truth.

As we face our own era of rapid technological change, growing inequality, and debates over the role of wealth in society, the Gilded Age offers both warnings and wisdom. The innovations of these industrial titans helped build modern America, but their excesses also sparked crucial reforms. Their philanthropic legacies demonstrate how private wealth can serve public good, while their monopolistic practices show the need for regulatory oversight. In their successes and failures, their virtues and vices, they mirror our own complex relationship with wealth, power, and social responsibility.

The streets of New York still echo with their influence – in the gleaming facades of Fifth Avenue, in the grandeur of Grand Central, in the institutions that bear their names. But perhaps their most important legacy is the ongoing dialogue they sparked about the proper balance between private wealth and public benefit, individual ambition and social responsibility, unfettered capitalism and necessary regulation. These conversations, begun in the Gilded Age, remain as relevant as ever in our own time of economic transformation and social change. As new fortunes rise and new technologies reshape our world, the lessons of these first American titans continue to resonate, challenging us to balance the creative power of capital with the demands of social justice and the common good.

A Final Word From The Author

Dear Readers,

I hope you've enjoyed this journey through America's transformative Gilded Age. As I conclude "Titans of the Gilded Age," I invite you to share your thoughts on these complex figures who shaped our nation.

The stories of Vanderbilt, Rockefeller, Carnegie, Morgan, and the Astors deserve not just to be read but discussed. Their legacies—magnificent cultural institutions alongside troubling labor practices, technological innovation alongside monopolistic control—continue to echo in our conversations about wealth, power, and social responsibility today.

I encourage you to visit the landmarks they left behind: Grand Central Terminal, Carnegie libraries, the Metropolitan Museum of Art, Newport's summer "cottages." These physical spaces offer tangible connections to an era that fundamentally shaped modern America.

If this book has sparked your interest, please consider sharing it with others who appreciate history's relevance to contemporary issues. I would be grateful to hear your perspectives through reviews, book club discussions, or social media conversations about how these Gilded Age lessons resonate in our own time of technological disruption and economic transformation.

Please consider leaving me a review on Amazon to allow us to share this amazing story of our history.

QR Code

Thank you for accompanying me through this fascinating chapter of American history.

With appreciation,

Margaret Ellis

References

1 https://biographics.org/cornelius-vanderbilt-americas-first-tycoon/

2 https://www.boldbusiness.com/human-achievement/bold-leader-cornelius-vanderbilt/

3 https://www.biography.com/business-leaders/cornelius-vanderbilt

4 https://en.wikipedia.org/wiki/Cornelius_Vanderbilt

5 http://www.thelatinlibrary.com/chron/civilwarnotes/vanderbilt.html

6 https://www.americanheritage.com/great-railroad-war-1877

7 https://www.cambridge.org/core/journals/journal-of-economic-history/article/decline-of-railroad-consolidation/787CE5D18051A0CF2DD3D54EE6662C71

8 https://www.shortform.com/summary/vanderbilt-summary-anderson-cooper-and-katherine-howe

9 https://www.lib.uiowa.edu/exhibits/previous/railroad/

10 https://commons.und.edu/cgi/viewcontent.cgi?article=2557&context=ndlr

11 https://www.supersummary.com/vanderbilt/summary/

12 https://oxfordre.com/americanhistory/display/10.1093/acrefore/9780199329175.001.0001/acrefore-9780199329175-e-931?p=emailAwQmfw2wWXE0o&d=%2F10.1093%2Facrefore%2F9780199329175.001.0001%2Facrefore-9780199329175-e-931

13 https://journals.sagepub.com/doi/pdf/10.1177/000271623417100122

14 http://tankona.free.fr/greenspan2018.pdf

15 https://laborguild.com/labor-history-blog-july-2024-the-great-railroad-strike-of-1877/

16 https://thearchitectureprofessor.com/2020/05/24/3-9-cornelius-vanderbilt-moves-into-railroads/

17 https://www.steelmuseum.org/railroadexhibit2015/barons_vanderbilt.cfm

18 https://www.khanacademy.org/humanities/us-history/the-gilded-age/gilded-age/v/the-gilded-age-part-1

19 https://en.wikipedia.org/wiki/Gilded_Age

20 https://ushistoryscene.com/article/progressive-digital-source-guide/

21 https://www.leadersthepodcast.com/blog/the-commodores-code-how-cornelius-vanderbilt-built-americas-first-business-empire/

22 https://en.wikipedia.org/wiki/HistoryofGrandCentralTerminal

23 http://daytoninmanhattan.blogspot.com/2013/02/the-lost-1871-grand-central-depot-42nd.html

24 https://www.planning.org/greatplaces/spaces/2013/grandcentral.htm

25 https://www.historyofjapaneseinny.org/exhibition_topics/grand-central-terminal/

26 https://metropolismag.com/projects/grand-central-terminal-100-years-of-a-new-york-landmark/

27 https://en.wikipedia.org/wiki/GrandCentralTerminal

28 https://www.6sqft.com/the-original-grand-central-was-a-site-to-behold/

29 https://advisorycloud.com/blog/uncovering-cornelius-vanderbilts-secrets-to-success

30 http://mastersinvest.com/newblog/2019/8/2/learning-from-cornelius-vanderbilt

31 https://www.ipl.org/essay/Cornelius-Vanderbilts-Impact-On-American-Business-873C98837411A98F

32 http://www.islandconnections.com/edit/vanderbilt.htm

33 https://study.com/learn/lesson/cornelius-vanderbilt-facts-railroads.html

34 https://thehustle.co/the-history-of-john-d-rockefeller-standard-oil

35 https://en.wikipedia.org/wiki/Standard_Oil

36 https://rockarch.org/resources/about-the-rockefellers/john-d-rockefeller-sr/

37 https://en.wikipedia.org/wiki/JohnD.Rockefeller

38 https://www.umw.edu/greatlives/2014/01/01/titans-of-the-gilded-age-rockefeller-carnegie-and-morgan/

39 https://guides.loc.gov/this-month-in-business-history/january/standard-oil-established

40 https://www.theellisschool.org/list-detail?pk=29083

41 https://www.ijnrd.org/papers/IJNRD2408132.pdf

42 https://www.learningtogive.org/resources/john-d-rockefeller-sr

43 https://www.studentsofhistory.com/gilded-age-robber-barons

44 https://www.investopedia.com/insights/history-of-us-monopolies/

45 https://jpt.spe.org/twa/the-antitrust-legacy-of-standard-oil-in-todays-world

46 https://billofrightsinstitute.org/essays/ida-m-tarbells-crusade-against-standard-oil

47 https://teachdemocracy.org/bill-of-rights-in-action/bria-16-2-b-rockefeller-and-the-standard-oil-monopoly.html

48 https://www.britannica.com/money/Standard-Oil

49 https://energyhistory.yale.edu/antitrust-and-monopoly/

50 https://www.ebsco.com/research-starters/history/standard-oil-trust-organized

51 https://www.econlib.org/archives/2013/01/rockefellers_ra.html

52 https://christianleaders.org/mod/page/view.php?id=30244

53 https://en.wikipedia.org/wiki/Elkins_Act

54 https://www.teacherspayteachers.com/Product/John-D-Rockefeller-The-Titan-of-the-Gilded-Age-9823673

55 https://online.maryville.edu/business-degrees/americas-gilded-age/

56 https://www.law.cornell.edu/wex/standardoilco.ofnewjerseyv.unitedstates_(1911)

57 https://historyincharts.com/the-legacy-of-the-breakup-of-standard-oil/

58 https://www.ebsco.com/research-starters/law/standard-oil-co-v-united-states

59 https://www.dividend.com/how-to-invest/the-complete-visual-history-of-standard-oil/

60 https://guides.loc.gov/chronicling-america-standard-oil-monopoly

61 https://supreme.justia.com/cases/federal/us/221/1/

62 https://ektinteractive.com/history-of-oil/

63 https://www.visualcapitalist.com/chart-evolution-standard-oil/

64 https://guides.loc.gov/oil-and-gas-industry/history

65 https://www.youtube.com/watch?v=npp2t3aVZBc

66 https://www.soonersaferhappier.com/post/6-organising-for-outcomes-from-steam-to-steel

67 https://endura-steel.com/the-bessemer-process-revolutionizing-steelmaking-and-industrialization/

68 https://d3.harvard.edu/platform-rctom/submission/carnegie-steel-building-a-modern-america/

69 https://www.thechemicalengineer.com/features/cewctw-henry-bessemer-man-of-steel/

70 https://www.mrs.org/docs/default-source/programs-and-outreach/imos-course/module-8/module-8---carnegie-creative-destruction-and-american-steel-2015-beta-wmrk.pdf

71 https://www.washoeschools.net/cms/lib/NV01912265/Centricity/Domain/1116/Period%206%20of%20Textbook.pdf

72 https://www.rotabroach.co.uk/blog/how-the-bessemer-process-changed-steel/

73 https://www.entrepreneur.com/leadership/what-andrew-carnegie-can-teach-entrepreneurs-about/483084

74 https://www.americanyawp.com/reader/16-capital-and-labor/andrew-carnegies-gospel-of-wealth-june-1889/

75 https://courses.lumenlearning.com/wm-ushistory2/chapter/industrial-growth-and-big-business/

76 https://keeganedwards.com/andrew-carnegies-empire-unveiling-the-business-strategy-behind-a-steel-titans-success/

77 https://www.britannica.com/event/Homestead-Strike

78 https://dp.la/primary-source-sets/the-homestead-strike

79 https://en.wikipedia.org/wiki/Homestead_strike

80 https://reimagineappalachia.org/remembering-the-homestead-strike/

81 https://www.pbs.org/wgbh/americanexperience/features/carnegie-strike-homestead-mill/

82 https://en.wikipedia.org/wiki/TheGospelof_Wealth

83 https://www.philanthropyroundtable.org/hall-of-fame/andrew-carnegie/

84 https://tnnonprofits.org/nonprofit-history-crash-course-the-hypocrisy-of-andrew-carnegies-gospel-of-wealth/

85 https://www.medalofphilanthropy.org/andrew-carnegie/

86 https://en.wikipedia.org/wiki/Andrew_Carnegie

87 https://richyoungpowerful.com/andrew-carnegie-the-gospel-of-wealth/

88 https://en.wikipedia.org/wiki/Carnegie_library

89 https://www.pbs.org/wgbh/americanexperience/features/carnegie-steel-business/

90 https://www.learningtogive.org/resources/carnegie-andrew

91 https://www.carnegie.org/news/articles/andrew-carnegie-legacy-support-public-libraries/

9 2 https://www.studocu.com/en-us/document/massasoit-community-college/world-history-i/robber-barons-vs-entreprenuerial-industrialists/21854309

93 https://americanlibrariesmagazine.org/2019/09/30/remembering-andrew-carnegies-legacy/

94 https://www.piton.org/andrew-carnegies-enduring-legacy-of-philanthropy/

95 https://blogs.loc.gov/inside_adams/2012/12/andrew-carnegie-man-of-steel/

96 https://en.wikipedia.org/wiki/J.P.Morgan

97 https://www.goodreads.com/book/show/1771523

98 https://guides.loc.gov/this-month-in-business-history/april/jp-morgan-born

99 https://www.britannica.com/money/J-P-Morgan

100 https://bankingjournal.aba.com/2017/10/j-p-morgan-railroad-referee/

101 https://www.ncpedia.org/anchor/growth-and-transformation

102 https://lithub.com/how-a-dangerous-exploitative-railroad-industry-created-j-p-morgans-fortune/

103 http://americainclass.org/wp-content/uploads/2013/03/WEB-Corporate-Consolidation-presentation.pdf

104 https://www.ebsco.com/research-starters/history/morgan-assembles-worlds-largest-corporation

105 https://www.americanheritage.com/deal-century

106 https://www.library.hbs.edu/us-steel/exhibition/the-founding-of-u.s.-steel-and-the-power-of-public-opinion

107 https://en.wikipedia.org/wiki/Panicof1907

108 https://www.ebsco.com/research-starters/history/panic-1907

109 https://carlsonschool.umn.edu/sites/carlsonschool.umn.edu/files/inline-files/Panic1907_1012.pdf

110 https://www.businessinsider.com/morgan-museum-and-library-tour-photos-art-collection-2019-10

111 https://www.thecollector.com/jp-morgan-legendary-americ an-art-collector/

112 https://www.investopedia.com/articles/economics/08/feder al-reserve.asp

113 https://www.stlouisfed.org/in-plain-english/history-and-pu rpose-of-the-fed

114 https://www.federalreservehistory.org/essays/federal-reserve -history

115 https://en.wikipedia.org/wiki/JohnJacobAstor

116 https://www.ebsco.com/research-starters/history/john-jaco b-astor

117 https://newbookrecommendation.com/books-about-john-j acob-astor-a-comprehensive-guide/

118 https://www.biography.com/business-leaders/john-jacob-as tor

119 https://www.legendsofamerica.com/we-johnjacobastor/

120 https://en.wikipedia.org/wiki/AmericanFurCompany

121 https://wsupress.wayne.edu/9780814343449/

122 https://buildingtheskyline.org/astor-index/

123 https://www.supersummary.com/astor/summary/

124 https://www.thepinnaclelist.com/articles/astor-family-legac y-rebuilding-new-york-gilded-age-grandeur/

125 https://en.wikipedia.org/wiki/WaldorfAstoriaNew_York

126 https://therealdeal.com/magazine/new-york-june-2008/joh n-jacob-astor-the-making-of-a-hardnosed-speculator/

127 https://thegreatestgrid.mcny.org/greatest-grid/john-jacob-a stor

128 https://en.wikipedia.org/wiki/CarolineSchermerhornAstor

129 https://www.geni.com/projects/The-Gilded-Age-The-400 -A-List-of-New-York-Elite-Society-Members-1870-1910/4490965

130 https://www.travelandculturesalon.com/blog/winter-gilded-age-new-york-city

131 https://www.immortalperfumes.com/storical/the-gilded-age-astors-vs-vanderbilts-pt-1

132 https://en.wikipedia.org/wiki/TheFourHundred(GildedAge)

133 https://en.wikipedia.org/wiki/HotelAstor(NewYorkCity)

134 https://en.wikipedia.org/wiki/Waldorf-Astoria_(1893%E2%80%931929)

135 https://www.garylawrance.com/blog/2020/9/10/john-jacob-astors-titanic-fifth-avenue-mansion

136 https://en.wikipedia.org/wiki/Astor_House

137 http://daytoninmanhattan.blogspot.com/2016/01/the-lost-1907-hotel-astor-1511-broadway.html

138 https://ephemeralnewyork.wordpress.com/tag/mrs-astor-mansion-fifth-avenue-34th-street/

139 https://visualizingnyc.org/broadway-and-ann/landmarks/astor-house/astor-house-1/

140 https://greenwichvillage.nyc/from-the-gilded-age-to-today-who-were-the-astors/

141 https://www.dvhd.org/blog/2024/3/4/queen-of-the-gilded-age-how-one-woman-changed-the-social-fabric-of-america

142 https://www.shortform.com/books/blog/astor-family-new-york.html

143 https://www.shortform.com/books/blog/history-of-the-astor-family.html

144 https://screenrant.com/gilded-age-mrs-astor-family-true-story-powerful-rich/

145 https://www.familyrootapp.com/blog/the-astor-family-history-a-legacy-of-wealth-and-influence

146 https://www.britannica.com/topic/Astor-family

147 https://www.businessinsider.com/presenting-a-history-of-the-astors-2012-4

148 https://www.youtube.com/watch?v=7A_BzGsSN4M

149 https://www.cbsnews.com/news/anderson-cooper-on-the-rise-and-fall-of-the-astor-fortune/

150 https://www.lovemoney.com/gallerylist/137029/how-the-astor-family-made-a-fortune-in-america-and-beyond

151 http://www.gildedageincolor.com

152 https://www.visitrhodeisland.com/editorial/post/exploring-the-gilded-age-rhode-islands-historical-landmarks/

153 https://en.wikipedia.org/wiki/Newport,RhodeIsland

154 https://newporthistory.org/about/newport-history/

155 https://www.discovernewport.org/about-newport/nine-coastal-communities/newport/

156 https://www.discovernewport.org/blog/post/gilded-age/

157 https://www.francisyork.com/blog/gilded-age-summer-cottage-in-newport-rhode-island

158 https://www.youtube.com/watch?v=kBwOjM_7OuY

159 https://www.visitri.com/state/mansions/

160 https://www.youtube.com/watch?v=H6u6IL51txQ

161 https://driehausmuseum.org/blog/view/gilded-age-new-years-traditions-champagne-and-celebrations

162 https://www.cityofnewport.com/Visiting-Newport/Eastons-Beach/Bathhouses/Rules-Regulations

163 https://www.wgbh.org/news/local/2024-08-21/newport-obsessed-over-the-vanderbilts-but-its-black-leaders-thrived-long-before-the-gilded-age

164 https://www.supersummary.com/the-gilded-age/summary/

165 https://www.rimonthly.com/catch-a-glimpse-into-newports-past-at-the-gilded-age-newport-in-color-exhibit/

166 https://travelingwithpurpose.com/secrets-of-gilded-age-newport-servant-life-tour/

167 https://www.thetravellinglindfields.com/2016/08/the-servant-life-tour-at-elms-newport.html

168 https://www.youtube.com/watch?v=6NubHMhqD3Q

169 https://www.bookishwayfarer.com/blog/the-elms-servant-life-and-house-tours

170 https://galeriemagazine.com/newport-gilded-age-mansions/

171 https://www.tripadvisor.com/AttractionReview-g60978-d181868-Reviews-RoughPointMuseum-NewportRhode_Island.html

172 https://travelswithtalek.com/visit-the-gilded-age-mansions-of-newport-rhode-island/

173 https://study.com/academy/lesson/gospel-of-wealth-definition-summary.html

174 https://www.carnegie.org/news/articles/focus-on-the-future-highlights-100-years-of-accomplishment-and-partnership-at-carnegie-corporation/

175 https://advisorycloud.com/blog/uncovering-andrew-carnegies-secrets-to-success

176 https://library.columbia.edu/libraries/rbml/units/carnegie/andrew.html

177 https://www.conversationsonphilanthropy.org/journal-contribution/the-gospel-of-wealth-and-true-philanthropy/

178 https://www.nps.gov/articles/carnegie-libraries-the-future-made-bright-teaching-with-historic-places.htm

179 https://philanthropydaily.com/the-peculiar-evolution-of-carnegies-libraries/

180 https://www.goodreads.com/list/show/92079.TycoonsofTheGildedAge

181 https://www.ourtownsfoundation.org/the-gift-of-a-public-library/

182 https://www.rockefeller.edu/about/history/

183 https://www.rucares.org/clinicalresearch/mission-history

184 https://www2.rockefeller.edu/ccts/about/history

185 https://en.wikipedia.org/wiki/Rockefeller_University

186 https://www.pbs.org/wgbh/americanexperience/features/gilded-age-mapping-gilded-age-new-york/

187 https://www.historyextra.com/period/victorian/war-of-the-operas-gilded-age/

188 https://collider.com/tthe-gilded-age-season-2-true-story-opera-war/

189 https://shamuskhan.wordpress.com/wp-content/uploads/2018/07/accominotti-ajs.pdf

190 https://library.fiveable.me/apush/unit-6/reform-gilded-age/study-guide/c8AtStJnup2hvLeHcZcC

191 https://adfontesjournal.com/miles-smith/progressives-and-the-bible-in-the-gilded-age/

192 https://www.rbhayes.org/research/hayes-historical-journal-gilded-age-evangelicals/

193 https://www.mexicohistorico.com/paginas/philanthropy-in-the-gilded-age-wealth-and-responsibility-1743291959.html

194 https://whorulesamerica.ucsc.edu/thecorporaterich.pdf

195 https://ephemeralnewyork.wordpress.com/tag/gilded-age-benevolence-nyc/

196 https://historum.com/t/the-gilded-age-captains-of-industry-or-robber-barons.90228/

197 https://www.nptuk.org/philanthropic-resources/giving-perspectives/the-new-gilded-age-changing-faces-of-big-philanthropy/

From The Author

Dear Reader,

When I first began researching the lives of America's industrial titans, I was struck by how profoundly their ambitions, innovations, and often controversial methods continue to shape our modern world. The skyscrapers of Manhattan, the railroads that connect our nation, the universities that educate our brightest minds, and even the structure of our economy itself – all bear the unmistakable imprint of these remarkable figures who transformed America from an agricultural nation into the world's leading industrial power.

In *Titans of the Gilded Age*, I have endeavoured to bring these extraordinary characters to life – from Cornelius Vanderbilt's ruthless business tactics to Caroline Astor's meticulous social engineering, from Andrew Carnegie's brutal labor practices to his genuine philanthropic conviction. Their stories reveal a crucial chapter in our national history, when the very foundations of modern America were being forged amid unprecedented economic transformation and social upheaval.

As we face our own era of technological revolution, growing inequality, and debates over the responsibilities of wealth, the lessons of the Gilded Age resonate with striking clarity. The questions that emerged during this pivotal period – about the concentration of wealth, the balance between private power and public good, and the proper role of government in regulating business – remain at the heart of our national conversation today.

It is my hope that this book will offer not just a window into a fascinating historical era, but a lens through which to better understand our present challenges and possibilities. The Titans of the Gilded Age were neither heroes nor villains but complex individuals whose legacies continue to shape our world in ways both profound and unexpected. Their stories remind us that in the ongoing American experiment, the tension between individual ambition and collective welfare, between innovation and equality, between private fortune and public benefit, remains as vital and unresolved as ever.

With gratitude for your interest in this remarkable period of American history,

Best Wishes

Margaret Ellis

Printed in Dunstable, United Kingdom

82450433R00107